Growing
into
Love

Before You Marry

Joyce Huggett

D0569911

InterVarsity Press
Downers Grove
Illinois, 60515

InterVarsity Press is the book-publishing division of Inter-Varsity Christian Fellowship, a student movement active on campus at hundreds of universities, colleges and schools of nursing. For information about local and regional activities, write IVCF, 233 Langdon St., Madison, WI 53703.

Distributed in Canada through InterVarsity Press, 1875 Leslie St., Unit 10, Don Mills, Ontario M3B 2M5, Canada.

All quotations from the Scripture, unless otherwise noted, are from the Holy Bible: New International Version. Copyright © 1978 by the New York International Bible Society. Used by permission of Zondervan Bible Publishers.

Cover photograph: David Singer

ISBN 0-87784-374-0

Printed in the United States of America

Library of Congress Cataloging in Publications Data

Huggett, Joyce, 1937-
    Growing into love.

    Includes bibliographical references.
    1. Love.   2. Marriage.   I. Title.
HQ801.H93   1982   646.7'7   82-18667
ISBN 0-87784-374-0

17	16	15	14	13	12	11	10	9	8	7	6	5	4
95	94	93	92	91	90	89	88	87	86				

Abbreviations

Bible references which are not taken from the
New International Version are quoted with the
following abbreviations:

GNB   *Good News Bible*, 1976
JB   *Jerusalem Bible*, 1966
LB   *Living Bible*, 1974

Preface

'Falling in love is a fantastic experience, but it presents a few problems as well.'

The speaker was a young friend of mine who had been unexpectedly swept off her feet by a member of our congregation. Her experience is not unusual.

Take Ken and Sue, for example. They fell in love in their second term at university. It seemed such a wonderful relationship. They really cared for one another, enjoyed each other's company and encouraged each other spiritually. But with two more academic years to complete, neither dared contemplate marriage. What were they, then – just good friends, or something more? How should they behave towards each other?

Or I think of Pete and Linda. They have already been going out together for four years. They are certain that they want to marry eventually, but Pete's mother insists that they are not suited and strongly advises them not to get engaged. Yet they know they are in love. They feel their love will result in marriage. How can they tell whether their feelings are right or whether Pete's mother has seen something they have missed?

And can anyone help Ron? He and Carolyn have been going out together for over a year now. Carolyn is convinced that God told her in a vision that she and Ron were to marry. But no voice from heaven seems to have given Ron the assurance he is seeking. Does this mean that he is less spiritual than Carolyn? Should he simply accept her vision without question?

Then there's Frank and Mary. They have a long engagement ahead of them. They are already finding that living with a powerful sex drive presents problems. How far can they go physically now they are engaged? Having erected realistic boundaries, how can they guard against the temptation to push these boundaries further and further out?

This book is an attempt to answer these questions and some of the others which young people in love frequently ask. It is therefore a book for all young people who are attracted by the opposite sex, as well as for those who are thinking of getting engaged and engaged couples who are preparing for marriage.

Marriage and engagement are frequently mentioned. This is not because I believe that boy-girl relationships which do not result in marriage are wrong. It is because I believe that the best time to crystallize your thinking about committed love – engagement and marriage – is *now*, when love has been newly awakened, or better still, before you even think of going out with a person of the opposite sex. People in love become delightfully disorientated. Very often they are unable to think very clearly. For this reason, I am not simply answering questions couples have asked me over the years. I am also asking you the questions I have put to couples who have come to me for help.

How to use this book

If you really want to benefit from reading this book, you will not just read it and put it down; you will use it as an assignment, working at the questions in italics.

A quick glance through the book will show you that there are plenty of these questions. There is no need to plough through them all. Be selective. But, of course, don't simply avoid the ones that look difficult or revealing!

If, like Ken and Sue, you are just good friends, it will be enough to discuss the questions which seem relevant to your relationship at the moment. But if you are seriously considering getting engaged, or if you are already planning your wedding, I would like to suggest an alternative way of responding to some of the questions in each chapter. *Do it in writing*.

Some couples avoid this method of communication, claiming that they cannot write well. Yet most couples become very excited about it when they have given it a try. This is not surprising, since writing has several advantages over talking.

Paper is very patient, for one thing, so it is never even tempted to interrupt your train of thought. Paper never looks bored, it can't cry and it never looks angry. Paper pays equal attention to men and women, so both partners have an equal say. If you really want to understand one another more fully, therefore, I strongly recommend that you try writing love letters to one another. Those letters will increase your knowledge of one another and this is vital, because knowledge is one aspect of real love.

A few couples insist that they cannot write. None the less, the kind of communication I am suggesting is vital to wholesome relationships. So if you can't write, talk.

Set aside half an hour and select one question. If you are writing, allow yourselves ten minutes to put down on paper how you are feeling about the question under discussion. Exchange letters. After you have read what your partner has written, discuss the contents of both letters. Then bring God into the feelings you have expressed by praying together.

Alternatively, if you are a non-writer, let one partner talk for five or ten minutes while the other listens, being careful not to interrupt. Then change roles. After you have each shared your innermost thoughts and feelings, you may find it helpful to discuss and pray over what has been said.

Does this sound like the dissection of love, like tearing off the wings of a fly to see how it works? It is not. Rather, it is the open sesame to understanding, knowledge and trust. Without these true love does not exist, but with them love not only survives, it blossoms.

Growth and love. That is what this book is all about. I believe that when a relationship grows, love grows. I also believe that love grows for those who work at it. That is why I am unafraid to suggest to you who are in love that you work at your love. I cannot guarantee that this will necessarily result in marriage with this partner. What I can assure you is that your understanding of love will deepen and if you do then decide to adventure into marriage, you will find yourselves growing ever deeper into love.

JOYCE HUGGETT
March 1982

1 So, You're in Love!

Can anyone deny that falling in love is a delicious feeling? It sends poets into ecstasies, song-writers into rhapsodies. Is it any wonder that the world resounds with echoes of love lyrics promising eternal passion?

This intoxicating feeling transcends class, culture and creed. It knows no bounds of age. As one sixty-year-old confessed to me recently, 'You never know when love will beckon.' For her, 'in love' for the first time, this call of Eros was a breath-taking encounter with beauty. It brought out the best in her. It made her generous, tender and self-forgetful.

When you fall in love you see the other person in a new way, open your heart to that person in a new way, desire that person in a new way. As C. S. Lewis observed, 'In one high bound [love] has overleaped the massive wall of our self-hood; it has made appetite itself altruistic, tossed personal happiness aside as a triviality and planted the interests of another in the centre of our being.'[1]

This magnificence of falling in love is laced with playfulness and laughter. When you fall in love you *feel* gloriously free to commit yourself to an eternal love with the loved one. And this invasion of an emotion which turns your life-style inside out seems to provide a natural springboard for commitment. But does it?

For some couples, clearly it does. They slip into engagement as easily as a diver slides into water. But others dither. And some couples never make the commitment to marry.

This turning back is not uncommon. Neither is it necessarily irresponsible. The decision not to marry may be prompted by the realization that falling in love is not the same as love. It is only the springboard which gives love a promising start. The love which cements marriage, that deeper, more lasting, more tranquil quality, might emerge from the euphoria, but it might not.

Romantic feelings

In fact, surrendering to passionate feelings can threaten love. It endangers the marital relationship if you place too much emphasis on this exhilarating feeling. For falling in love *is* a good feeling. But it is still a feeling, and feelings cannot last. Take the preoccupation with the loved one, for example. This longing to be together, to communicate by letter or by phone, cannot last in its intensity. Or take the powerful waves of physical attraction, the sexual stirrings, the feverish excitement of being together. These feelings change, mature and deepen. But that is not to say that love becomes dull or stale. The quality of love grows calmer yet even more exciting and longer lasting.

Do I seem a killjoy by emphasizing the short duration of romantic feelings? My aim is not to rob you of your joy but to be realistic. Infatuation *is* short-lived. As C. S. Lewis observed, this is no bad thing. 'Who could bear to live in that excitement for even five years? What would become of your work, your appetite, your sleep, your friendships?'[2] And who would pay for the phone calls, the postage and love's extravagant trinkets?

In our more rational moments we may smile at these overwhelming feelings, but we must not despise them nor minimize them. And never assume that they are hidden from God. On the contrary, they stand out from the pages of the Bible. In the Song of Solomon there is portrayed the playfulness of erotic love (Song 1:4), the languishing of unsatisfied desire (2:5) and the force of sexual attraction (*e.g.* 1:2; 2:1–7; 4:1, 9).

God understands these feelings. It was He who created us with the ability to be swept off our feet by a person of the opposite sex. But it is He who advises us, through the writer of Proverbs, to set a watch over the affections of the heart. 'They influence everything else in your life' (Pr. 4:23 LB).

Feelings govern actions. We see this in the kind of person who seems to thrive on chasing love. Each time they 'fall in love' they are convinced that *this* time it is the real thing. *This* love will last for ever. They therefore invest time and energy in the relationship only to find that when the initial tidal wave of erotic feeling ebbs away, 'love' retreats. They are left beside dwindling pools of hope. Fullness becomes emptiness.

But ceasing to *feel* in love need not mean ceasing to love. Psychologists warn us that feelings of infatuation last from three to thirty-six months. Does that mean that couples are then left stranded on a love-less beach? Of course not. Marriage is a whole. Infatuation is only one segment; a zestful relationship between the sexes has so many more. Friendship, companionship, emotional and spiritual oneness all contribute to the togetherness which creates a complete marriage.

What motivates your relationship: infatuation, kisses and cuddles? Is there something more? If so, what?

These questions are compulsory for any couple who have fallen in love. But love is blind, so it is not easy to respond to them with honesty. If you work at the assignments in each chapter of this book, however, I believe you will gain a more accurate picture of your relationship. You will become aware whether the foundations for Christian marriage are being laid.

'But we're just friends'
'The foundations for Christian marriage'? Maybe you are reading this book, not because you hear wedding-bells, but because you have fallen in love and are searching for the answer to such pressing questions as, 'How far should we go physically in expressing our love for each other?'

There is no definitive answer to this question, but chapter 9 of this book suggests principles to bear in mind as you construct a code of behaviour which seems right to you; ways of keeping your own rules without hurting yourself or your partner.

Maybe your relationship raises other questions. 'If we don't plan to marry, should we allow our friendship to continue?'

In my opinion there is great value in cultivating friendships across the sex barrier. Men need the warmth of female love to draw out their masculinity, and women need the understanding of men to draw forth their full femininity. The danger comes when two people fall in love and form an exclusive relationship. When lovers begin to neglect other friendships spend all, or most, of their time together and rarely, if ever, include others in their twosome, an exclusive relationship exists. It is selfish and harmful.

It is harmful for two reasons. First, single people need many friends of both sexes if life is to become rich and varied. Second, what happens when your romantic attachment has outworn its glamour? You and your partner are in danger of finding yourselves isolated from those who would have befriended you, but whom you have chosen to ignore. That is unwise and unloving. It is unloving to neglect the friends who need you as much as you need them. It is unloving to your partner who could suffer an indescribable loneliness if your relationship does not work out. It is also unloving towards yourself and your own needs.

Is it wise, then, to form 'attachments' at all? Don't the disadvantages outweigh the advantages?

Undoubtedly there will always be pain in loving. Even so, I believe two people in love can make an enormous contribution to one another's growth if the relationship is handled wisely. Take Liz, for example. Her relationship with Len was starry-eyed, short-lived and ended painfully, but it helped her to accept her womanhood and that gift did not disappear with Len.

When a relationship is characterized by kindness, encouragement and challenge, both partners should grow as a result of the love poured forth. Kindness is the caring which wants to communicate, 'I am all for you.' Encouragement is the quality which draws out the full potential in another, gently urging, 'You can do it.' And challenge is the love which persuades a person to reach beyond his/her old limitations. I am not talking here about sexual love, but the love which enables the loved one to rise above a fear, to turn away from the sin of bitterness, jealousy or resentment, or to break off self-destructive habits. Are you contributing to your friend's growth in this way? And love between Christians always seeks to bring the loved one nearer to God.

Should you, then, pray and do Bible studies together if you are just good friends?

Praying together and studying together brings an inevitable closeness and of course this is not wrong. But there are two pitfalls to avoid. First, don't confuse spiritual oneness with emotional intimacy. They overlap but they are not the same. Second, if these two strands do become entangled, beware of abandoning your own spiritual pilgrimage at the same time as you move away from this friendship.

Why might it become necessary to move out of this partnership? It sometimes happens that what started as a brother-sister relationship develops into something more for one of the persons involved. This is one of the risks you take in developing friendships across the sex divide. If it happens, the only sensible thing to do is to talk it over. This won't necessarily be easy, but it is better to be honest now than to suffer the pain of a broken relationship when you have invested all your hopes in it.

'A broken relationship.' Is this inevitable if you fall out of love? I don't think it is. Couples who have been in love, who then realize that their relationship will not result in marriage, can so set one another free that they are able to form a deep friendship even when one or both of them starts to go out with someone else. Such friendships are often long-lasting and of great value because the qualities which attracted you to one another in the first place do not die with the demise of the courtship. Even when sexual attraction has evaporated, therefore, closeness can continue.

Closeness *can* continue, but you may need a temporary break from one another before you find yourselves able to bridge the inevitable gap which exists between a romantic relationship and a platonic one. During the time of separation, you should both avail yourselves of the healing the Lord gives for the hurts which so often accompany this kind of loss. Only when you have both been touched by God in this way will you be capable of receiving one another back, ready to build a new kind of friendship.

So how do you know whether this relationship will result

in marriage? Or as one young friend of mine put it, with a note of exasperation, 'In the Christian life we are always being told not to rely on feelings. But what else is there to go on with relationships?'

A deeper understanding of yourself, the nature of love and God's purpose for marriage are aids to the objectivity he was searching for. So, then, what is the purpose of marriage?

The purpose of Christian marriage

Man made in the image of God (Gn. 1:26) possesses an innate ability to give love, to receive love, to communicate with others, to co-operate with others. This free-flowing love is expressed most intimately in marriage. In fact the one-flesh union seems to have been built on the relationship which existed between the Father and the Son before the world was made: a relationship of unfailing love (Jn. 17:24). Just as marriage, as described in Genesis, sprang from divine love, so Christian marriages are rooted and grounded in Christ. God Himself holds the relationship together. He feeds it with vigorous love. This love is not so much a feeling as an orientation. It is love in action.

This love is defined in 1 Corinthians 13: 'Love is patient, love is kind...It always protects, always trusts, always hopes, always perseveres' (vv. 4, 7). And this passage warns us what love is not. Love 'is not rude, it is not self-seeking, it is not easily angered, it keeps no record of wrongs. Love does not delight in evil but rejoices with the truth' (vv. 5–6).

Taking these verses as your guide, is your love real?

How do you know?

This definitive ode to love embraces all kinds of Christian loving, not just marital love. But in Ephesians 5:21ff. Paul places marriage under the microscope, bringing it into sharp focus.

The prototype for Christian marriage is the relationship between Christ and His bride, the church. 'Husbands, love your wives, just as Christ loved the church and gave himself up for her...husbands ought to love their wives as their own bodies' (Eph. 5:25, 28). This is a superlative form of loving which is concerned for the other's total good. It implies that marriage is a deep, unique, maturing partnership. It is intended to last for a lifetime (v. 31). It is based on exclusive commitment. It involves the abandonment of each person to the other. This permanence and intimacy call for a high degree of self-sacrifice from both partners. It is a self-giving which mere feelings will not support. Love's demands can be met only by those who genuinely love. Those who are merely 'in love' will shrink from the high cost of loving.

The high cost of loving

But what is the cost involved in forming a lifelong relationship with one you love deeply? Surely couples will pay any price for the prize of marital love?

If this were true, the incidence of marital breakdown would be less frightening than it is. Statistics suggest that one couple in three in Britain, more in the United States, find that the feelings which attracted them to one another before marriage are insufficient to withstand the demands of a lifelong partnership. So how do you know whether you are ready to make the commitment to marry?

The next eight chapters of this book are designed to help you discover the answer to that question. But if you want a quick test, take this quotation from Michel Quoist:

> To love does not mean to seize the other for your own fulfilment but rather to give yourself to the other for his or her own fulfilment. You are ready for the experience of genuine love when your need, and especially your desire to give, is more compelling than your need and your desire to get...Don't simply ask yourself: Is this love? Rather ask yourself: Does my love rest upon renunciation, self-forgetfulness and self-giving?[3]

Renunciation, self-forgetfulness and self-giving. These are the ingredients of the love from which healthy marriages are created. Do they describe the love you have for your partner?

Does your love model itself on Ephesians 5:21ff.?

Or are you attempting to establish a Christian relationship by aping the behaviour and customs of the world?

The strong bias to self-centredness which is characteristic

of each of us presents a barrier to marital love as God intended it. Selfishness destroys love. Couples therefore have a great need to find in Christ the resources they need if they are to give love to anyone, including their partner in marriage. Only the Spirit of Jesus who transforms our attitudes and behaviour patterns can make us equal to the sacrifice demanded. Even then it takes years for Him to change selfish human beings into persons who put the interests of others first.

To love, therefore, is costly. It frequently hurts. C. S. Lewis put it well:

> To love at all is to be vulnerable. Love anything and your heart will certainly be wrung and possibly be broken. If you want to make sure of keeping it intact, you must give your heart to no-one, not even to an animal.[4]

Count the cost of loving. Count the cost of marriage. This challenge to count the cost is not new. Jesus placed it before us in a different context. 'Suppose one of you wants to build a tower. Will he not first sit down and estimate the cost to see if he has enough money to complete it? For if he lays the foundation and is not able to finish it, everyone who sees it will ridicule him, saying, "This fellow began to build and was not able to finish"' (Lk. 14:28–30).

This love, if you allow it to continue, will disrupt your life-style, your attitudes, your entire self. Is that what you want? Do you want to marry? Do you want to form a lifelong union with this partner? Is your match a good one? These are the questions we go on to examine. If these are the questions you are asking, I suggest that you approach this book, not as something to read, but as an assignment to be worked at. In the Preface I suggested practical ways of selecting and responding to these questions. So if, like me, you normally ignore Prefaces, perhaps you would turn back and read mine now!

And what if you have no intention of marrying this partner? The Preface suggests ways in which you, too, may benefit from this book so that your understanding of one another will deepen.

How do you feel about the prospect of sharing your innermost thoughts and feelings with one another?

Notes for chapter one

1. C. S. Lewis, *The Four Loves* (Fontana, 1963), pp.104f.
2. C. S. Lewis, *Mere Christianity* (Bles, 1969), p.86.
3. Michel Quoist, *The Christian Response* (Gill and Macmillan, 1965), pp.33 and 110.
4. *The Four Loves*, pp.111f.

2 The Choice: Married or Single

'I really want to marry. But if it's better for the kingdom of God, I will stay single.' The young man who said this is an eligible bachelor already much used by God. It sums up the conflict felt by many Christians. Should I marry? Or can I be of greater service to God if I remain single? Is celibacy a higher calling than marriage?

The pressures are not only spiritual ones. Practical considerations make the choice a difficult one.

'We've talked about everything under the sun concerning ourselves, our ambitions and fears, our attitude to each other and our attitude to marriage. We've had violent arguments, we've had really good times. We've even had one or two of our precious weekends together so busy that we've hardly seen each other. I feel as though I've had all the fantasy beaten out of me – and I still want to marry him. Mind you, I reckon it's a high-risk venture, to use some business jargon.'

The decision to marry is indeed risky. But there is an element of risk in remaining single, too. It is perplexing because it is not a straightforward choice between good and evil. Rather, it is a choice between good and good, and that is much more complex. To remain single is good. For some people it is the pathway to wholeness. To marry is also good. God calls most people to pursue the vocation of marriage. Yet doesn't Paul claim that celibacy is to be prized more highly than marriage?

The advantages of singleness
Paul certainly accentuates the advantages of singleness. He reminds us that the unmarried person enjoys freedoms which are denied to married people. This detachment of singleness frees a person to serve God in any place and at any time. His

devotion to God *can* be undivided (1 Cor. 7:32–35). It can be greatly used to extend God's kingdom.

When we worked in partnership with an unmarried vicar, we appreciated Paul's point of view. Our vicar gained access to places we did not. He worked late into the night with students, uninhibited by a wife nagging him if he arrived home in the small hours. No babies interrupted his morning prayer.

I am aware that the grass is always greener on someone else's patch. So let a single person spell out the joys this freedom brings:

> Freedom to travel, freedom to follow a career, freedom to develop and expand personal interests, freedom to widen one's circle of friends, freedom to choose between company and solitude, freedom to grow as an individual, freedom to give time, money and talents to whatever cause pulls at the heart-strings. The list could stretch on and on.[1]

I am not suggesting that the personal freedom of the single person is unlimited. Many have dependent relatives to care for in a sacrificial way. But, as Margaret Evening warns, 'there can be so much freedom in the single life....that one has to guard against selfishness.'[2]

Some people value the benefits of singleness so highly that they are prepared to forgo the pleasures of marriage altogether. They feel like the girl in the children's poem:

> If no one ever marries me –
> And I don't see why they should,
> For nurse says I'm not pretty
> And I'm seldom very good –
>
> If no one ever marries me
> I shan't mind very much;
> I shall buy a squirrel in a cage,
> And a little rabbit hutch...
>
> And when I'm getting really old,
> At twenty-eight or nine,
> I shall buy a little orphan girl
> And bring her up as mine.[3]

Such independence and self-indulgence were not the characteristics Paul applauded in 1 Corinthians 7, however. The celibacy which Paul advocated demonstrates the ultimate in self-sacrifice. This self-renunciation is prepared to burn out for Christ. It is motivated by love for Christ. This love comes from God and reaches out for Him. It is a zeal which is sturdy enough to withstand being stripped of all advantages. As someone put it to me rather dramatically: 'I vowed that naked I would follow the naked Christ.'

This is the singleness which Paul would promote. This is the life-style which he labels 'better' than marriage. Is this the singleness you would choose if you decided not to marry?

Is your present life-style consistent with your intellectual response to that question? How?

The disadvantages of singleness

Given the choice, most people choose marriage. They know that the sacrifices required from the single person are exacting. Paul Tournier writes, 'No, it is not easy for a woman, for any woman, to accept celibacy. A spiritual miracle is absolutely necessary, without which the supposed acceptance is only chagrin and repression.'[4] The renunciation of sexual intimacy is traumatic. This is equally true for men and women.

But sexual deprivation is only one of the disadvantages of singleness. It is accompanied by a deeper problem. Some single people suffer an incurable loneliness. A single woman in our church explained how it catches you unawares, like the jab of a thorn when you are picking roses. We were bunching flowers for Mothering Sunday when she explained how she both loved and hated the moment when the children presented the posies to their mothers. She rejoiced in the happiness radiating from them. But she dreaded the wounding this inflicted on her. 'It reminds me that *I* belong to no-one; *I* matter to no-one.' This bitter-sweet experience is reflected, too, in a wistful prayer of Michel Quoist:

Lord
  It's hard to love everyone and to claim no one.
  It's hard to shake a hand and not want to retain it.

It's hard to inspire affection, to give it to you.
It's hard to be nothing to oneself in order to be everything
    to others...
It's hard to seek out others and be unsought oneself.[5]

This aloneness is deepened on occasions when married people
delight in their togetherness. As couples travel to church
together, exchange news after a busy day, luxuriate in their
unspoken oneness as partners, the single person remains
alone. Loneliness stings.

This sting is aggravated by the stigma society attaches to
singleness. The assumption is made that all single people
want to marry; that they are without status until they do.
The playful teasing at weddings, 'It will be your turn next,'
often rubs salt into an already festering sore. The implication
is that the single person is missing out on life. And some are.

But, clearly, others live fulfilled lives. They serve God with
undivided loyalty and devotion. These single people are an
inspiration to any married person. They demonstrate that
wholeness comes, not through marriage, but through being
in complete alignment with the will of God.

Are you prepared to renounce marriage if that is what God
asks of you?

How do you feel about remaining single?

The advantages of marriage

To claim, as I have done, that there are disadvantages in
remaining single implies that there are advantages in being
married. Can anyone deny this? The Creator Himself
exclaimed, 'It is not good for the man to be alone' (Gn. 2:18).
It was for this reason that He instituted marriage. What are
the benefits of the lifelong relationship established between
two people in marriage?

From the beginning, the marital relationship became a
place of healing. Just as this was true for Adam when the
wounds of solitude were soothed by Eve (Gn. 2:23), so it is
one of the characteristics of healthy marriages today. Couples
bring old hurts and insecurities to their marriage. As a new
pattern of loving is established, those scars and bruises are

gradually touched and healed over by God through one another. Then they lose their restrictive power. Marital love often frees persons to love others. Marriage can therefore double a person's effectiveness in the service of God.

A couple's usefulness is enhanced by their completion of each other and their complementarity. As at the beginning, marriage is that point where two sexually incomplete but compatible persons of the opposite sex unite. In fusing their bodies, they create a whole, new, third person, 'us'. There is no loss of identity in this fusion. Rather, this combination of resources is an investment from which both gain. The dividends are mutual strength, encouragement and support. As these 'two solitudes protect and touch and greet each other', to borrow Rainer Maria Rilke's phrase, they, in turn, find themselves able to reach out to others. This is love's overflow. It is one of the reasons why Christian marriages are greatly used by God.

For marital union is not just sexual. Christian marriage can be that place where two loves meet; the human and the divine. The author of Genesis unveils this mystery (Gn. 1:28–29). Adam and Eve met the Lord God who talked to them, instructed them and walked with them in the garden.

The joys of family life, moreover, are frequently applauded in the Old Testament. It does not even mention a word for 'bachelor'. It would seem that marriage was the norm in those days.

Then what does the New Testament teach about marriage? Jesus places a strong emphasis on the sanctity of the marital bond. He reiterates the responsibility couples have to leave the past behind so that they are free to unite to form a one-flesh relationship. Jesus not only acknowledges marriage; He blesses it with His presence (Jn. 2), rescues embarrassed newly-weds with a miracle, and promises that couples who work at 'leaving and cleaving' will, gradually, become one (Mt. 19:4–6).

And although in one place (1 Cor. 7) Paul suggests that celibacy is 'better' than marriage, this is not a complete summary of his teaching. Clearly celibacy is a gift for some and in the face of impending persecution, and in the light of the imminent return of the Lord, could be described as 'better' than marriage. But let us not lose sight of Ephesians 5:21–32, where Paul speaks of marriage in superlatives. Marriage is about mutuality and sharing; it is about person-making. As Jack Dominian reminds us, Ephesians 5

> is the acme of spiritual vision. Nothing finer nor more exalted is to be found anywhere else....Here St Paul, following the prophetic imagery of the covenant between God and his people, goes on to affirm that the union of two in one between husband and wife is a union with a relation that parallels, imitates and participates in, so far as is possible, the closeness and love exchanged between Christ and his bride, the Church. The significance of this new revelation lifts marriage for all time into the realm where absolute love reigns, the love of Christ for his Church.[6]

Moreover, Paul owed much to a Christian couple, Aquila and Priscilla. They supported him and worked alongside him as he founded the church in Corinth. They also discovered the potential in Apollos, instructing and encouraging him.

The Bible's view of marriage seems to be of two persons interlocking. They are designed to fit into one another, like a two-piece jigsaw. This unit in turn slots into the supportive framework of God's love. It is the divine love which holds the pieces together. The partners are the objects both of the other's love and of God's love.

This is the great advantage of marriage. This love sustains the woman who needs to be valued, respected and comforted. It also nurtures the man whose need is for a companion, someone who will be all for him, who will be on his side in times of stress. Virginia Satir expresses it succinctly. In marriage:

> I make you more possible,
> you make me more possible,
> I make us more possible,
> you make us more possible,
> and us makes each of me and you more possible.[7]

Thus you, me and 'us' all benefit. Or, to borrow a Dean of

Durham's phrase, marriage is that place where 'two "I's" become a "we"'.

This love includes fearlessness, trust and versatility. It is rooted in belonging, in knowing. It is therefore a magnificent platform from which to reach out to others. The unity which comes from the cluster of unions of marriage has to overflow in effective Christian service.

But it is at this vantage-point that the disadvantages pinch. And marriage has many disadvantages.

The disadvantages of marriage

Paul Tournier summarizes the problem: 'Marriage is not just a question of sex. It is also a school for self-forgetting.'[8] And who wants to forget 'number one'? Who *wants* to sacrifice selfish desires? That is the last thing most people want. And so, while the rewards of marriage attract, its demands repel.

Marriage is offensive to some because it requires complete renunciation of personal independence. But independence and self-actualization are twentieth-century gods. We are instructed to worship them. What then is to happen?

What does happen is catastrophic. People use marriage as a means of self-discovery: 'The intimacy of the marital relationship and the joys of parenthood will draw out *my* full potential, to help *me* to discover who I am.' But this attitude imperils a relationship which demands the abandonment of purely personal goals, ambitions and satisfaction. This attitude results in disillusionment. It is as Jesus warned, 'Whoever wants to save his life will lose it' (Lk. 9:24).

Then what is to happen? Marriage must be viewed as the 'school of self-sacrifice' and a paradox must be recognized. It is those who allow their needs and concerns to be swallowed up in an enterprise which rises above selfish desires who discover the meaning of life, the truth about themselves and the rewards of marriage. Those who actively pursue self-satisfaction rarely find it. When the limitations of marriage are accepted, when we resist fretting about 'me' and 'my needs', a miracle takes place.

At least, that is how it has been for us. When we least sought them, personal growth, fulfilment and emotional wholeness began to creep up on us. They came to stay. They arrived as a gift from God.

This wholeness is a gift we offer to the other. It is not something we grab for ourselves. That is why marriage chafes. The point is that the reason for living changes course when we marry. If I choose to marry, I decide to renounce my right to happiness, usefulness and comfort. Instead, I adopt a new set of priorities. These priorities insist that, from now on, I will seek to *give* love to my partner. I will make the other happy.

Do you feel called to the vocation of marriage with this partner?

Are you prepared for the re-orientation of priorities which this vocation demands?

What sacrifices are you prepared to make to ensure that your love works?

I have tried to show in this chapter that celibacy is not a higher calling than marriage. Rather, it is different. Single people are not necessarily more useful to God than married people. They bear fruit in different ways, achieve wholeness in different ways and learn the art of selflessness in different ways. For self-actualization is not to be realized in marriage or in singleness. Its source rests in God. Each Christian needs to discover this truth. The secret of my identity is rooted in God. Richard Jones puts it well:

> God alone is the ultimate good. He is the source of all value, all goodness, all worth. All other 'goods' are derived from Him. To worship and adore Him is the supreme end of our existence, besides which nothing else is of importance.[9]

If we are to discern this call and act upon it, we shall have to discard all that is not of God. Our peace of mind rests in Him. And if we truly seek His will, we shall find it. But the discovery of His chosen path calls for obedience. It demands sacrifice. It leads to a closer union with God. It will only be God who knows what we leave behind and what we choose to sacrifice. It will only be God who replenishes the inner joy which makes the choice of a high-risk proposition possible.

Do you want to marry?

Why?

How do you feel about this statement: 'Marriage is not the best way of life for everyone – but the way of self-giving love is'?

Notes for chapter two

1. Margaret Evening, *Who Walk Alone* (Hodder and Stoughton, 1974), p.218.
2. *Who Walk Alone,* p.220.
3. From 'If No One Ever Marries Me' by Sir Laurence Alma-Tadema, from *Realms of Unknown Things* (Garnstone Press).
4. Paul Tournier, *Escape from Loneliness* (SCM Press, 1962), p.78.
5. Michel Quoist, *Prayers of Life* (Gill and Macmillan, 1968), p.50.
6. Jack Dominian, *Christian Marriage* (Libra, 1977), pp.24f.
7. Virginia Satir, *Peoplemaking* (Science and Behavior Books, 1972), p.127.
8. *Escape from Loneliness,* p.85.
9. Richard Jones, *How Goes Christian Marriage?* (Epworth Press, 1978), p.109.

3 How Can We Be Sure? Getting to Know You

God's guidance sometimes comes in a blinding flash. 'I met John at a conference and I just knew that I had met my other half.' But more often God nudges us on to His planned pathway with a growing awareness that a course of action is right. And whether you enjoy the assurances of a 'heavenly vision' or whether you awaken slowly to a certainty about your partner, there are things you need to know about each other if you want to be sure that you are compatible. Intimate knowledge of the other is part of the preparation of pre-engagement.

This preparation has nothing to do with the planning of dates, the making of cakes or the choice of clothes. It centres on the growth of your relationship. To ignore this work is irresponsible; to participate in it deepens real love, strengthens healthy relationships and increases a couple's chance of building a stable marriage. Lovers love to talk about their love. For this reason, this preparatory work is nothing more than love's 'beautiful curiosity'.

John felt this curiosity. His love for Ruth prompted him to say, 'I love you so much, I want to know everything about you.' So they started from the beginning. Each related his/her personal history for the other.

This is a useful way to establish a strong partnership. It helps you understand one another. And as Paul Tournier reminds us, 'One who feels understood feels loved, and one who feels loved feels sure of being understood.'[1]

But where do you begin? How can your understanding of one another grow?

Background and family

It is widely recognized today that who we are and what we

have become depend not only on the present but on the past. In all probability, you each bring at least twenty years of past experience to this relationship. Joy and pain are concealed in those years. You can help one another towards a deeper understanding of the mystery of who you really are by lifting the veil from your past.

Take your experiences of family life, for example. If you are in your twenties, the people who have influenced you most so far will probably be your parents. They will have moulded your life by their presence, and by their absence.

How would you describe your relationship with your mother?
And your father?

If you enjoyed a close and warm relationship with them in your early years, you were privileged. It was a good start to life. As a result, you are probably the sort of person who makes relationships easily. Unless, of course, this closeness became claustrophobic during the teen years. Teenagers need to extend their horizons. They want the benefits of affection without its demands. Parents who fail to appreciate this frequently smother their growing offspring. If you felt stifled by your parents, you may be cautious in the way you relate to others. Perhaps you have become the sort of person who sometimes yearns for intimacy but who equally demands space? There is nothing wrong with a warm, loving, outgoing person who sometimes needs to be alone, but it is important that you recognize that this is a need for you.

But suppose that your relationship with your mother, or father, or both, was impoverished, that they have been more absent than present in your life, that you came from a broken home or your parents are divorced? It could be that your ability to trust another person in an intimate relationship has been impaired. If your partner understands this before you marry, his/her acceptance of you could heal over some of the emotional wounds which you have probably covered over and even forgotten.

There is value, therefore, in trying to evaluate your relationships with your parents.

How do you feel about their parenting?
Is there anything you would like to change?

This should not become an excuse for wallowing in self-pity. Nor is it an opportunity to apportion blame. Rather, this awareness provides an occasion for you to express your feelings.

What are your *needs as you form close relationships?*

Closely linked with your family is your background. Unlike couples in the past who often attended the same school, worshipped in the same church or lived in the next street, you may not share identical backgrounds. This could be enriching, or it could be destructive. Even when differences in background appear to be slight, they frequently irritate. If cultural differences are big, as in racially mixed marriages, the strain can become intolerable. It is not just a question of racial or class prejudice. We need to see the problem in practical terms. The adjustments required of couples in any marriage are considerable. They frequently place a relationship under strain. This is accentuated when the individuals have inherited and adopted conflicting social and cultural patterns.

Describe your background. Evaluate it.

Do you want to perpetuate your parents' values and life-style? Or are there some things you will gladly abandon? What are these things?

Make a careful note of your similarities and your differences.

If it is true that differences which seem attractive before marriage may become irritants when you have to live with them, how do you plan to live with your differences?

Are you being realistic?

Intellect and recreation

If differences in culture and class grate, discrepancies in intellectual ability also cause chafing. You have only to watch couples sitting together in a restaurant to see how bored some people have become with each other. After a few years of marriage, the relationship seems stale. There are many contributing factors. One is that the gulf which separates them intellectually is too wide to bridge. This leads to frustration. One partner will start a conversation, and because their differences are so great, the other feels inferior. None of us enjoys feeling small. It feels threatening. It pushes partners into arguing. These people are always in competition. They use dialogue to 'put each other down'. Or else conversation collapses and the whine is heard, 'My husband doesn't tell me anything,' 'My wife doesn't talk to me any more.' Partners who cannot talk to each other find someone else to confide in. This is where much marital infidelity begins.

In healthy marriages, on the other hand, the compliment is voiced, 'You grow more interesting every day.' This is part of the adventure of marriage.

Try to establish your intellectual compatability by reminiscing about your school-days. Assess them.

Do they provide happy memories? Or sad?

Were you a success at school? Or a failure?

Who recognized your worth during your school years?

Did anyone topple your self-esteem?

When you have compared your school-day experiences, try to measure your intellectual 'fit'.

How much disparity is there?

Do you interest and stimulate each other? Or do you find your partner boring?

This interest in the other spills over into your leisure time. Part of the enjoyment of marriage rests in learning to relax together. This includes sexual intimacy, but it is so much more. Relaxation extends to shared interests and common values. Each of these makes a contribution to satisfying relationships.

Review the past again. When you were little, how did you relax?

What kind of recreation did you pursue in your teens?

When there are no pressures of any kind now, how would you choose to unwind?

Are there hobbies and interests you both enjoy?

If there are, recreation becomes communion. It unites. But if you always need to compete when you relax, or if sport always separates you, your relationship will suffer.

Are you each prepared to take up new interests for the sake of this togetherness?

What might they be?

Space and togetherness; spiritual closeness

That is not to say you must always be together. Some people need to re-create in solitude. There is nothing wrong with solitude. An intimate relationship between two people asks for togetherness *and* space. This desire for space need not be interpreted as withdrawal from the loved one. Rather, it must be viewed as withdrawal *into* beauty, silence or rest. Partners who love one another learn to safeguard one another's privacy. This protection deepens the quality of the relationship. Each contributes new strength to the partnership.

Periods of rest and relaxation punctuate phases of creativity. We are creatures of rhythm, designed to enjoy work and leisure. Just as relaxing together is unitive, so sharing common tasks with your partner in marriage adds strength to the relationship. For this reason, couples who work together often enjoy an intimacy which others envy. This closeness is brought into being by the mutual shouldering of responsibility and the pooling of different strengths. When you combine your complementary gifts in a project, it produces a sense of achievement. The feeling of togetherness this provides is felt when two Christians unite to serve God in specific ways, such as running the Youth Group, entertaining the lonely, or opening their home for a house group. It also occurs when the couple throw themselves into the mundane, humdrum tasks of life: decorating a room, or creating a garden, as well as in ways which are usually labelled 'spiritual'.

What kind of mundane tasks do you enjoy doing together?
How do you express your creativity with each other?
How might your partnership be used by God?

That last question assumes the importance of spiritual closeness. Young people often ask whether Christians should marry non-Christians. The Bible emphasizes that believers should avoid harnessing themselves 'in an uneven team with unbelievers' (2 Cor. 6:14 JB. See Am. 3:3). This prohibition is not the command of a spoil-sport God. It is the loving advice of the heavenly Father whose legislation always safeguards our best interests. When two Christians marry they become soul-friends. Prayer unites them. It is not only church leaders who are urging Christians to marry Christians. Sociologists also sound the warning that religiously mixed marriages are precarious, whereas a shared faith holds persons together.[2]

But why is this spiritual oneness so valuable? Its value lies in the positive benefits which derive from friendship with God.

There is the asset of prayer, for one thing. Charlie Shedd, a Christian marriage counsellor, helps us to understand what a vital resource this is: 'I have never had one couple or one member of a marriage come to me with their troubles if they prayed together. (There were a few, perhaps a dozen, who said "We used to!")'[3]

Praying introduces a sense of the eternal into the relationship. It is the focus of your work for God. It is the place where the needs of the relationship, relatives, the world, may be lifted to God. In prayer, too, you may each enjoy an encounter with God.

This prayer need not be verbal. Charlie Shedd recommends silence. He suggests that, at the end of the day, couples 'slip their joined hands into the hand of God' and sit silently in His presence. Some find this helpful. Others have a need for the beauty of words. One couple I know end each day by reading a short, liturgical service together. It is their way of expressing their adoration for God. Others read prayers which, inspired by the Holy Spirit, have been written down by other people. This is sometimes a Psalm, Jesus' 'prayer book'. Or you might read a modern prayer. How you pray is your choice.

Do you pray together?
Do you want to?
How will you go about it?

Prayer is only one of the privileges Christian couples enjoy. When they unite, they can be caught up in the great commission of Christ to herald and extend His kingdom. Is there a finer project in which to involve your partnership? The exciting thing is that when two Christians donate their complementary gifts to the marriage and to God, He multiplies their effectiveness. Their usefulness as married people is greater than the total sum of the contribution they each make. Thus the marriage is enriched, the community is touched and God's kingdom is furthered.

Christians who are going the same way with the living Christ profit, too, by submitting themselves to a Lord who is wiser than either of them. This yielding of love to Love holds the relationship together, refines it and gives it purpose and strength.

How do you feel about your spiritual oneness?

Emotions and forgiveness

The unity which we discover in one another when we both owe allegiance to Christ does not replace the need for emotional intimacy. As John Powell puts it,

> My emotions are the key to me. When I give you this key, you can come into me, and share with me the most precious gift I have to offer you: myself.[4]

This communication of feelings is vital to healthy marriages. But most people have difficulty in unveiling hopes and fears, dreams and fantasies, tastes and values, particularly in the presence of their loved one. It requires patience, time and plenty of courage; but the rewards are rich. Each individual gradually feels accepted, affirmed and valued. That is the pathway to wholeness.

Are you prepared to work at the difficult art of communication?

Think carefully before you answer that last question. It has been claimed, and in my opinion rightly, that 'a relationship which spells closeness also spells conflict'.[5] How do you two cope with conflict? Do you quarrel heatedly? Or perhaps you freeze? Do you heap blame on each other? Maybe you are both mature enough to recognize that each of you must accept some of the responsibility when conflict arises.

All good marriages include an element of conflict. It cannot be avoided. Couples who tell you they never quarrel are either not telling the truth or they live such separate lives that there is little opportunity to clash. And Christians do not escape this conflict.

Do you forgive the other quickly or reluctantly?

Is this forgiveness based on the need to give love or just the desire for a cuddle?

How do you express that forgiveness?

Habits

Personal habits create some of this marital conflict. Despite all the jokes, after twenty years of marriage I *still* leave the top off the toothpaste. It's irritating. And these idiosyncrasies are magnified if your sense of humour fails to harmonize with your partner's. Then quirks of habit become occasions for nagging. And 'a woman's scolding' (or a husband's nagging) 'is like a dripping gutter' (Pr. 19:13 JB).

Can you accept each other's habits?

Acceptance is not ignoring faults; it is recognizing them without magnifying them. It is easy to assume that habit patterns don't matter, but habits which faintly jar before you are living together become much more threatening after you are married. And the glib, 'The Lord will iron out the creases' mentality is, in my view, too simplistic.

If you simply read this chapter, it will do little to heighten your awareness of your partner, your relationship or yourself. You may still remain unsure whether you are compatible or not. This understanding can only grow if you will commit yourself to work at the questions, preferably writing down your reactions for your partner to read.

Is this work necessary for those who are sure that their relationship was 'made in heaven'? I believe it is. If you are certain that God brought you two together, this exploration of your attitudes, thoughts and feelings will not only increase that certainty, it will also unfold for you the goodness of God in giving you to each other. If you are already cemented by love, surely you will want that desire to increase? This happens with knowledge, not ignorance; reality, not fantasy.

And if you are certain of your love and the purpose of God for your relationship, it makes sense to become wise stewards of His gift. Stewardship involves actively promoting that which God entrusts. If you believe your relationship is His gift, working at the art of togetherness is one of the ways of maximizing your potential.

As you apply your creativity to the work suggested in this chapter, you will discover where your similarities lie. These will strengthen your relationship. Your differences will also be highlighted. These could divide you; but they might add zest to your marriage. It depends what you do with them. That is the subject of the next chapter.

Notes for chapter three

1. Paul Tournier, *Marriage Difficulties* (SCM Press, 1967), p.28.
2. For instance, Jack Dominian, *Marital Breakdown* (Pelican, 1968) and *Marital Pathology* (Darton, Longman and Todd/British Medical Association, 1979).
3. Charles Shedd, *Letters to Karen* (SCM Press, 1968), p.137.
4. John Powell, *The Secret of Staying in Love* (Argus, 1974), p.78.
5. Quoted by Howard and Charlotte Clinebell, *The Intimate Marriage* (Harper and Row, 1970), p.95.

4 How Can We Be Sure? Examining Our Match

What is a good match? Is it two identical colours? Sameness. Or is it contrasting colours? Difference. 'Good match' describes them both. Does this apply to relationships as well as things? I believe it does.

Sameness in relationships brings comfort. It offers couples the kind of contentment swans seem to enjoy, the luxury of gliding across a still pond together. But most people want contentment laced with spontaneous adventure. That is why men and women fascinate one another. The exploration is not just sexual. There are emotional differences which fill relationships between the sexes with intrigue. Men and women are therefore capable of drawing out the highest and best in one another.

Virginia Satir, a family therapist, makes this claim:

> I believe that two people are first interested in each other because of their sameness, but they remain interested over the years because of their differences. To put it another way, if humans never find their sameness, they will never meet; if they never meet their differences, they cannot be real or develop a truly human and zestful relationship with one another...Any two human beings, no matter what their similarities, are going to find differentnesses. And *vive la différence*! Think how boring and sterile life would be if we were all the same! It is difference that brings us excitement, interest, and vitality. It also brings a few problems![1]

These problems cannot be ignored, as other counsellors are quick to point out. Jack Dominian, for example, repudiates the claim that 'opposites attract'. He claims that considerable research has failed to substantiate the theory, although he admits that it is an interesting one. He adds an important warning. If couples do decide to marry on the basis of their differences, they must be aware of the dangers. The chief danger is that the needs of one partner may be matched only by the opposite and complementary needs of the other; the balance created is a delicate one. Any slight change in circumstances could upset the precarious nature of the relationship. A partnership established chiefly on complementarity might not possess enough resources to hold the marriage together.[2]

Sally and Graham discovered the wisdom of this advice. When they married, Sally was immature; shy, insecure and dependent. She found a father figure in Graham. 'I like it when he treats me like a baby.' But Graham's love helped her to gain in confidence. Sally's needs changed. Now she needs, not a solid, dependable figure, but a stimulating companion. She has started to strive for a greater degree of autonomy. Graham, however, felt more comfortable with the original 'father role'. He feels threatened by the liberated wife he watches emerging from the chrysalis of their marriage. A comfortable relationship has become a tempestuous one. The delicate balance has indeed been upset.

Problems like these incline some counsellors towards the view that opposites should not attempt to live together. 'I listen to the sound of their voice. Voices tell you what people are like. A slow voice reflects a phlegmatic personality. Quick speech characterizes an active person. If their voices are incompatible, I advise them not to marry.'

But are these conclusions right? I question them. Certainly too many differences create instability. But some differences are inevitable and we must not run away from them. We must learn to cope with them.

Review your relationship. As you responded to the questions in the last chapter, were you more conscious of your differences or your similarities?

What attracted you to one another in the first place, sameness or 'differentness'? Is there a balance?

How are you compatible?

What is compatibility? Not feelings. As C. S. Lewis warned, 'Many unhappy and *predictably* unhappy marriages, were love matches.'[3]

When your spiritual, emotional and practical similarities unite you so that you feel at ease with each other, compatibility exists. This harmony, this meeting of whole persons, furnishes the relationship with the necessary resources to use differences to advantage. Then, 'otherness' does not spoil a relationship. It enriches it.

Making differences work for a relationship
Differences enhance a relationship when you make them work for you. Take social differences, for example. Robin is a friendly person when you know him, but if you met him at the back of the church, he might seem rather gauche. On the other hand Mary, his wife, is an outgoing person. She puts people at ease immediately. At first, Robin used to feel threatened by Mary's ability to make firm friends quickly. Did this mean she was 'better' with people than he was? Gradually he realized that their gifts were complementary. When they pooled them, their usefulness was more than doubled. He now allows Mary to make the initial contacts. He knows he is not excluded so he also joins in. Together they create a relationship which is far more valuable than either of their separate contributions. This is the exciting thing about complementarity. It completes persons and increases their wholeness.

One way to make differences work for you, then, is to recognize where you complement each other. Take a look at the wholeness this offers to your relationship and to other people. This healthy view of complementarity encourages you to applaud your partner's 'otherness'. You can glory in it. You might even encourage it.

This encouragement could open new doors for you. If a book, a hobby or a place is of interest to your partner, then there must surely be something of value there which is worthy of exploration. If you take the trouble to find out what this merit is, you extend the limits of your own backyard. This makes life an adventure. At least, that is what we have found. When I fell in love with an aeronautical engineer, now my husband, I raised my head from the history books I had pored over and became conscious of the greatness of the God of space. David's 'otherness', his preoccupation with space technology, opened new vistas for me. It continues to do so. Similarly, my work with deaf children introduced him to the fascination and pain of the world of the disabled. His world was also enlarged.

Blending opposites is a rewarding pastime.

Take a look at your partner's differences. How do you feel about them?

Can you approve them, affirm them and promote them? Or is your reaction purely negative?

If you view your partner's differences as threats, or if you determine to reform him/her, you should examine your relationship with great care. If you cannot accept this 'otherness', or if you dislike the differences intensely, you need to assess your partnership with the help of an older person. Where areas of similarity provide a high degree of overlap, there might be sufficient resources between you to transform problems into blessings. But if your differences outnumber your similarities your relationship might, in fact, be a misfit.

Carol and David wondered if they were misfits. Carol's parents said they were. Carol is a warm, outgoing person. David is shy. This reserve camouflages kindness, sensitivity and vulnerability. They trained as students together; that is how they met. Carol achieved a first-class degree, while David failed to complete the course. Now they are both in business where David is heading for promotion. Carol loves fellowship groups, singing and praying aloud. David is quieter. He goes with her to the group but it is not his spiritual wavelength. He prefers solitude. Should they marry?

As David and Carol talked about their background, intellectual and spiritual compatability and the possibilities of recreational togetherness, the situation seemed to clarify. They knew they were attracted to one another. They perceived many similarities which added strength and stability to these feelings. But they did not ignore the differences. They laughed at some and confronted others. Most of their differences, they feel, are the 'otherness' which could lead to wholesome complementarity. They know it will be hard work, that they cannot change each other. But each is allowing God to change his/her attitudes through prayer. They have decided to marry.

James and Pauline, on the other hand, came to the painful conclusion that they really did not fit. James, an only child, loathed babies. He was an academic and his career was all-important. He 'knew' that babies would interrupt his professional chances. When he asked Pauline to marry him, he made it clear that he never wanted children.

But Pauline loved babies. She had decided that she wanted four. She loved James; at least, she was 'in love' with him. But she also wanted children. She knew that, for her, motherhood was an essential part of marriage.

Faced with the prospect of a lifelong union, they made their decision and separated. We all saw the pain and felt some of it. Two people rarely part painlessly. But their decision was right. There were huge areas of incompatibility which would have caused continuous chafing. The immediate issue, babies, was the peg on which they hung disparity of values, attitudes and expectations. These would never have been resolved. The conflict would have proved unbearable.

If you do not 'fit' you must split. It is the only responsible course of action but it is a painful one. Couples who begin to prepare seriously for marriage and who then decide to go their separate ways because they do not fit, suffer a mini-death. This sense of bereavement is experienced, too, by couples who choose to separate for other reasons. Bereavement means loss. Most of us do not cope easily with the loss of a loved one whether through death or separation. It is for this reason that a certain amount of 'grief work' must be done.

'Grief work' is the process of coming to terms with the changes which take place within you when a loved one is removed. Psychiatrists remind us that there are five phases to this procedure. First you have to accept the numbness. Your feelings seem to be frozen and are no longer a part of you. The numbness wears off and you move into the phase of 'sighing', when any reminder of your loved one brings a stab of pain. Crying is a third, essential part of grief work. Don't hold back your tears, therefore. They are a language which will express your anguish in a way words cannot. And don't be surprised if you feel angry. The person suffering from loss frequently experiences an angry or depressed stage before he/she moves into the final stage of grief work; the ability to say goodbye to the loved one and to walk away, to re-negotiate life on a new set of terms. Eventually it does become possible to start life afresh without the one you loved, but this process cannot be rushed, so you must be patient with yourself.

And what if you do fit? Biologically, you fit because you are different, 'other'. Hence, husband and wife become one flesh. Marriage leaves room for certain spiritual, emotional and practical 'otherness'. But the sexual fit apart, your fit is most comforting when you are similar. Greatest strength comes from sameness. You must decide whether your togetherness will accommodate the exhilarating tension of your differences. Or are the differences already troubling you?

How can you tell?
Discovering whether you fit cannot be done in a hurry. This is one of the reasons why the longevity of the pre-engagement period is important. This is a period of learning and is vital to your relationship. You need plenty of time to learn to understand one another. Understanding is one of the prerequisites of marital love. It comes with hours of patient talking and listening. That is why couples who marry after a brief courtship often have a precarious introduction to marriage. To rush into marriage is so unwise that Jack Dominian maintains that couples should take at least a year to grow together before they marry. Walter Trobisch offered the same advice.[4] Of course, we can all point to the exceptions, the people who plunged into marriage and appeared to weather the turbulent adjustments well. But the exception is not the rule. Most couples *need* at least a year in which to begin the essential work of pre-marital adjustment.

This creative effort, without which no marriage succeeds easily, should form a vital part of pre-engagement. It is another reason for delaying marriage until you have 'summered and wintered' together, to borrow Trobisch's phrase. This gives ample time to assess your relationship.

Take the problem of similarities and differences, for example. How are you to begin to assess whether your partner's habits irritate unless you have known him/her for an extended period? How can you evaluate whether your partner's strengths complement your own unless you have begun to combine them at a time when you are not pressurized?

And there is another reason for a leisurely courtship. It provides the space you need to adjust to the problems of conflict. Intimacy creates conflict. How do you cope with conflict and quarrels? Do you blame one another or placate each other? Do quarrels lead to frequent storms and the painful upheaval of separation? Or can you face conflict realistically? If you both forgive and seek to understand the other's point of view, you are well on the way to adjusting to marital conflict. Your relationship is strong. But if you are unable to face conflict you should not consider an early marriage. This is courting disaster.

Doubts are another indication that you should pause. The hope that 'it will be different after we are married' is untrustworthy. It may be different. It will probably be worse. It will be worse because, if his eating habits annoy you now, they will be magnified when you have to live with them. And worse, they may find a home in *your* children. They will be worse because, if you dislike the way she dresses now, she will seem positively slovenly in her curlers. Doubts must be confronted. Until they become relative certainties you should not marry. You do not 'fit'.

And if you fail to create a fit you owe it to yourselves to flash the amber light. Parents and friends may ask embarrassing questions. They may well be disappointed. But their disappointment is less important than your security. A little care now could save you the heart-break of a broken marriage. I am not saying you can be absolutely certain that you will be compatible for the rest of your lives. Walking by faith includes not knowing. I am saying beware of embarking on marriage in the light of glaring discrepancies and huge doubts.

Perfect match?
We consider the question of doubt again in the last chapter.

In deciding whether you create a 'perfect match', three more things remain to be said. First, there is no such thing as a 'perfect match'. Personalities never fit perfectly. Couples in books 'live happily ever after'. Couples in real life make good marriages only through hard work.

Second, your motivation to work at this relationship will be reduced unless you have erased unrealistic fantasies from your imagination. This applies to both men and women. It was a blockage for Val.

She used to dream of the handsome curate she would marry one day. He would be her spiritual leader and she would help him in his work. They would serve God side by side. Then Val fell in love with Paul. But Paul was not a curate, and he was not particularly handsome. What is more, this civil servant had been a Christian only a few months when they met. But they were in love and they got married. Val still secretly 'blames' Paul for not being the strong Christian of her dreams. Her fantasies prevent Paul from becoming the husband God meant him to be. Until she lets go of the fantasy, she traps Paul in an unrealistic mould. She stifles his growth.

Men, I find, also conceal a mental short-list. Peter's list described the glamorous, sylph-like figure of the girl he would marry. When he married Sue, he kept the secret list. Unfortunately, the list did not tally with Sue's measurements. At times he uses his fantasy to taunt his wife, inflicting deep hurt.

Do you have a short-list? Does it contain the 'essential characteristics' of your future partner? Burn it. Erase the memory. This is an act of the will which requires humour and prayer. It frees you to offer unconditional love to your partner, thus setting him/her free to be the person God made him/her to be.

Third, this freedom to love rarely matures before the twenties. Plenty of statistics support this claim. Research shows that 40% of teenage marriages end in divorce.

The reason for this is not difficult to understand. Two students meeting in their first term at university might appear to make a perfect match. But a university career is a period of re-evaluation, of assessment and maturation. Tastes change, values change and views change. It follows that the eighteen-year-old 'fit' will also change. It may become a misfit. This is not because young people are fickle. Rather, it is because young adulthood involves rapid growth. You may choose to ignore the high incidence of marital collapse among the under-twenties. But is it wise to do so? Jack Dominian concludes that marriage for the under-twenties is 'a high risk proposition'. 'Every piece of research has shown that youthful marriages are extremely vulnerable.'[5]

Of course, this is hard for the young person who longs for marriage. It is especially difficult for Christians who struggle to live without sexual gratification in a climate where most of their friends indulge freely in sexual experimentation. The temptation to throw caution to the wind, to marry the first person who comes along, will always be present. But any divorced person will tell you that marrying the wrong person is much more painful than remaining single. Some people dread that the world will end before they have found the right partner. They need to ask for a special touch from God to cope with the frustrations of singleness, to wait until a suitable partner comes across their path.

When you assess your match, you should be free from pressure from parents or from your partner. If your partner does urge you to marry sooner than you feel ready, it is worth asking whether it is you he/she loves, or simply himself/herself. Growing into the realization that you really do 'fit' is fun. There is a sense of luxury about leisurely love. As a young friend of mine wrote: 'I remember those summer evenings when we sat in the car watching the sun set over Viewpoint Hill. It was there that we talked. We started at the beginning and just went on until there was no more to tell. Then we knew that we were ready for marriage. We already "belonged". And where that belonging was incomplete, we both knew that we wanted to work to make the other happy. And so we made our decision to marry.'

Notes for chapter four

1. Virginia Satir, *Peoplemaking* (Science and Behavior Books, 1972), pp.138f.
2. See Jack Dominian, *Marital Pathology* (DLT/BMA, 1979), p.16.
3. C. S. Lewis, *The Four Loves* (Fontana, 1963), p.100.
4. Walter Trobisch, *I Married You* (Inter-Varsity Press, 1972).

5 Hopes and Expectations

'What do you hope for from marriage?' I put the question to a girl, Gill, who had recently announced her engagement. She looked coy, blushed a little and then confessed that she hadn't thought that far ahead. 'I'll just take it as it comes, I guess.'

But Gill is a social worker. In her work, she sets herself clear goals. In developing her union with God, she also plans the way ahead with meticulous attention to detail. Why, then, this reluctance to clarify the expectations with which she approaches that most vital relationship, marriage?

This reluctance to express the high hopes one places on the marital relationship is common. But hopes and expectations need to be voiced. Giving them expression has three main advantages. First, this unveiling of desire enables your partner to assess whether he/she can begin to match your hopes and meet your needs. Second, it is as you place your dreams side by side that you see more clearly where you are compatible and where you complement each other. But there is a third reason. Clarifying your marital ambitions provides the relationship with a sense of purpose. When you each declare your deepest longings, it becomes clear what you two are setting out to achieve. This adds zest to love.

Why do you want to marry?

Why do you want to marry this partner?

Why do you want to marry at this stage of your life?

Respond to those questions in writing. Examine your replies and consider their implications. Then begin to investigate the ways in which you plan to meet each other's needs. Can you fulfil the other's hopes? Perhaps some of your expectations are totally unrealistic? If they are, a wise couple recognizes that either some of their cherished longings must be placed on one side or the relationship must be terminated. Is your partnership deficient? Or are you demanding more from your marriage than a human relationship can reasonably offer? If you are unable to unravel the answer to those questions for yourselves, seek advice.

If you discover that you are over-optimistic, learn to laugh at the unreasonableness of your demands. Laughter heals. It paves the way for realism, as one group in our church discovered recently.

This group was disintegrating. The cause, they claimed, was lack of good leadership. What did they require of their leader? As each person in the group expressed his/her expectations of the group leader it became clear that the archangel Gabriel himself would not have qualified. This healthy ventilation of unreasonable hopes caused amusement. It was liberating. It resulted in a more accurate assessment of the purpose of the group, affirmation of the person who had struggled to hold them together and the construction of a step-by-step plan for the future.

No couple can plan the route through the whole of marriage before the adventure has even begun. Circumstances change, tastes change and requirements from life evolve. It is possible, however, to plot short excursions into life. If you are serious about your relationship, it is advisable to map out the path which will best take you through engagement and the early months of marriage. Setting yourself realistic guidelines at this stage could result in months of fulfilment as you watch each target being reached and passed.

This sense of achievement is vital. It is important because, at a time when expectations of marriage are higher than ever before, marriage as an institution seems to be less stable than formerly. Thus the satisfaction level does not match the high level of expectation. This leads to disillusionment. This disillusionment is one of the chief causes of marital breakdown today. And this creeping disease often begins early in a relationship.

Is marriage unstable? Are high expectations wrong? What are the expectations couples bring to marriage?

What are your hopes?

Marrying for love

Most couples marrying today claim that they are 'marrying for love'. This is a comparatively recent phenomenon. In the past, parents or marriage-brokers would have created the match. Love was expected to emerge from these 'arranged' marriages, but love was not the basis on which the marriage was constructed. If the bonus of love never materialized, the couple was still held firmly together by clearly-defined roles. As long as the husband fulfilled his functions well as provider, protector and bread-winner, he was considered to be a good husband. Meanwhile his wife would meet his domestic and sexual needs and devote herself to his children. This earned his approval and made her a good wife. Since the expectation of life was considerably shorter than today, a husband and wife could co-exist reasonably happily. Even if they never learnt to love each other, they probably loved at least one of the children. They could therefore relate through their offspring.

But now, all that has changed. Marriages can last longer. Most couples marrying today may reasonably expect to live together for fifty years or more. Their relationship could outlive the years when children remain at home. And there are other changes. Love is no longer considered an optional extra. It is the essential foundation on which thriving marriages are built. This love is required to span all aspects of the relationship: social, recreational, emotional, intellectual, economic and domestic. Its benefits should enrich both partners. Couples are no longer held together by function. They are cemented by love.

It is hardly surprising that marrying for love has swept away the traditional patterns of marriage in recent years. Richard Jones, in his fascinating survey of marriage, opens up the extent of these changes. They are recent. In 1950, for example, 'husbands and wives put a lot of emphasis on moral and economical qualities: a sense of humour, fairness, faithfulness, moral qualities, personal qualities, intelligence... being a good cook.' Nineteen years later there was a noticeable swing:

In 1969 the emphasis had been shifted to psychological qualities: understanding, love and affection, patience, equanimity, shared responsibilities and interests and, emphatically for the husbands, being a good mother.[1]

This shift in emphasis has continued. Today couples rarely, if ever, marry a partner who will simply be an efficient executant of a clearly-defined role. They marry because they love each other. This loving includes liking. It is characterized by mutual understanding, emotional sustenance and caring. The prize of love is the personal growth which results from each partner helping the other through personal and marital problems. This love union is warm, close and tender.

Marrying for love provides the setting for the gems of friendship, shared harmonious living and the sexual fulfilment of both partners. Clearly this kind of marriage, sometimes called companionship marriage, offers richer rewards than its traditional counterpart. In traditional marriage, there was little companionship. The need for togetherness went largely unacknowledged. And although the sexual needs of the husband were sometimes met, the wife's desires were frequently disregarded. It was as though she hadn't any. Companionship marriage, on the other hand, highlights the relational nature of marriage. Love makes inroads into every part of the relationship. It is this love for which most couples crave.

The problem

So what is the problem? The problem is that companionship marriage offers seemingly unlimited advantages. It also makes costly demands and you cannot enjoy the benefits without paying the price of 'that special richness', love. And there are other complications, too.

The newness of companionship marriage contributes to the apparent instability of the marriage relationship. Stereotyped patterns of marriage offered a definitive way of life. The husband went out to work, controlled the finances and made major decisions. His wife cleaned the house, cooked the meals and looked after the children. But companionship marriage acknowledges no such conclusive boundaries. This is both liberating and perplexing. It is liberating because it gives scope for creativity, exchange of certain roles and experimentation. This is fun. It is perplexing because there are few rules to this new game. Couples must make up their own and that is not as easy as it sounds.

It is difficult because love is not always 'doing what comes naturally'. Love has to be learnt in the hard school of experience. We all know the theory of love, but it takes hours of patient practice to translate this theory into a life-style. Moreover, couples are required to compose the rules of their game before they have gained the experience of mature loving. This creates more problems.

There is another snag. Most couples marry for love, but few ever define what they mean by that altruistic statement. It might mean that you want to pour out love for your partner; to increase his/her self-esteem, improve his/her welfare, and to convey that knowledge which all persons need to hear, 'I am lovable! I don't have to do anything or be anything but myself. I am valuable and worthwhile in myself.'[2] On the other hand, you might not be so desirous of giving love as of receiving it. 'I want you to love me, to meet all my dependency needs, to quench my insatiable need for attention.' Perhaps marrying for love combines these two extremes? But it follows that the person whose main aim in marriage is to give love in generous measure will invent a far less selfish set of rules than the person whose horizons do not extend beyond self's needs and whose aim in marrying is to grasp love greedily

And there is another difficulty. Although we convince ourselves that companionship marriage is more rewarding than the outmoded customs we have discarded, and although we recognize that flexibility *is* richer, even more biblical, than stereotyped marriages, past patterns haunt us. They hold us in their ghostly grip. 'I still feel guilty when I leave Mike to cook his own supper.' 'I feel *I* ought to organize our finances, although I know Sheila would be more efficient.' These persistent voices from the past prohibit harmonious sharing unless couples discuss the rules of their game. This discussion should continue until you are sure that your proposed life-style coincides with your partner's. If it doesn't the game will collapse around you.

Begin to write the rules for your partnership.
What do you expect from your husband/wife?
What are your feelings about fixed roles and headship and submission?
Chapters 12 and 13 place the spotlight on these subjects.
Here we go on to consider further hopes and expectations.
Love is not the only reason why people marry.

Marrying for happiness
Some couples marry for happiness. But what is happiness? It is a mirage. Its delights are transient. One moment they are there, then the dazzling beauty vanishes. Do you really want to marry for happiness, that will-o'-the-wisp which is destroyed by adverse circumstances? The answer to that question might be Yes. In our wisest moments each of us knows that the tantalizing conclusion of all good fairy-stories, 'They lived happily ever after,' *is* a fairy-tale. Yet this romantic fable does not lose its appeal. The dream lingers. We would like it to come true for us, but the solemn truth is that marriage is not for happiness, it is for wholeness. Wholeness leads to something deeper than happiness, an inner, indestructible joy. This lasting joy is nurtured in secure relationships. It needs constancy, dependability and predictability for its growth. That is why Christian couples can experience an unassailable joy. This joy is a gift which originates in the heart of God. His gift is safeguarded for life; pain, sorrow and temptation are powerless to touch it. As Jesus said in a different context, 'Your hearts will be full of joy, and that joy no one shall take from you' (Jn. 16:22 JB).
How do you plan to help your partner reach his/her full potential through engagement and the early months of adjustment to marriage?
What does he/she need from you?
Wholeness is brought about through trust, acceptance, receptivity and prayerfulness.
How will these qualities feature in your marriage?
The real meaning of love is to procure your partner's wholeness.
How will you give yourself to that task?

Marrying to escape

This self-giving is one of the essential ingredients of love. But some people marry, not so much for what they can give as for what they hope to receive. These hopes, too, should be aired before marriage. They are not necessarily wrong, and since they are a part of you, your partner has a right to hear them and to measure his/her ability to meet them. Take, for example, the desire to escape from loneliness. Surely this is biblical?

At creation God observed that it was not good for man to be alone. But marriage is about relationships, creativity and the activity of love. Love desires not so much its own good as the welfare of the loved one and others. If you marry only to escape from the aloneness of singleness you may find that you have a complex assignment on your hands which makes untold demands. If you are not willing actively to promote your partner, you should not marry. By 'promote' I do not mean that partners should pressurize one another to succeed, nor should they idolize one another. Rather love for the other will involve drawing out the best in him/her; the promotion of realistic personal growth.

But, of course, marriage does alleviate aloneness. David Mace puts it well:

We all need friends. Of all the experiences which men and women can encounter, loneliness is one of the most dreaded. One of our deepest human needs is the need to love and be loved. Of course that need can be satisfied apart from marriage. But the close and intimate life together of husband and wife has always provided the ideal solution for most people. Sharing their resources, their plans, their hopes, the married couple grow into a fellowship of warm affection and mutual trust which becomes more and more precious to them as the years go by.[3]

In avoiding loneliness, are you also prepared to share your resources, your plans, yourself?
Do you feel this will be easy or difficult with this partner?
How will you begin to support the other emotionally?

Pauline discovered the hard way that marriage cannot be used only as an escape route. She was in love with a married man when she met James. She had been praying that God would send her a partner, because she longed to escape from the agony of an adulterous relationship. James seemed to be the answer to her prayer. They married. But Pauline brought impossible demands into their relationship. Her desire was not to promote James; it was to seek consolation for herself. Their marriage fractured.

How are you planning to promote each other?
What have you to give to one another?

Marrying for status

Some single people long for marriage, not just for the companionship – though that is an important consideration – but for status. Despite the clamour of feminists in recent years, there is still a supposed stigma attached to the single state. Marriage appears to provide a higher status. But for the Christian this should not be a contributing factor. Status is something to be relinquished, not highly prized. Our goal in all things should be to obey God, whom our souls love, and to follow the path which He unfolds for us. If this path leads to marriage, that is our highest vocation. If it is singleness with the stigma attached, this is the calling which will lead us most directly to Himself, the source of joy.

When parental pressure is exerted, this obedience to God needs to be recalled. Parents, friends and relatives perpetuate the myth that the only road to fulfilment leads through marriage. This is not the truth. Many fulfilled, joyous and fruitful Christian people demonstrate the falsity of this claim. It is possible to love deeply and to be loved in return without being married. But, of course, for the Christian, singleness involves celibacy, and many people marry because sexual oneness with a person of the opposite sex is a passionate yearning. This desire should transcend the biological urge. It should symbolize the longing for the true union of hearts which is one aspect of comradeship. It is one definition of that quaint phrase 'one flesh'.

Is it wrong, then, to go into marriage with high expectations of the sexual relationship? I believe that high hopes are both healthy and right. Sensitive, effective and satisfying sex forms the heart of wholesome marriages. One of the keys to satisfying sex is communication. Couples need to learn to lay on one side their reluctance to talk about sexuality. The next five chapters of this book are designed to open the lines of communication on this confused subject.

But perhaps you bring hopes and expectations to your relationship which have not been mentioned in this chapter? What are they?

When Virginia Satir asked this question, this is what her research revealed:

> Women's hopes centred around having a man who, of all people in the world, would love only them, who would respect and value them, and would talk to them in such a way as to make them glad to be women, who would stand by them, give them comfort and be on their side in times of stress.
>
> Men have said they hoped for women who would see that their needs were met, who enjoyed their strength, their bodies, regarded them as wise leaders and who would also be willing to help them when they expressed their needs....As one man put it, he wanted someone 'who is all for me. I want to feel needed, useful, respected and loved – a king in my own house'.[4]

Of course, we shall not all echo those hopes. Honest as they are, some of them are selfish.

How do you feel about the desires expressed?

Notes for chapter five

1. Richard Jones, *How Goes Christian Marriage?* (Epworth Press, 1978), p.32.
2. John Powell, *The Secret of Staying in Love* (Argus, 1974), p.19.
3. David R. Mace, *Whom God Hath Joined* (Epworth Press, 1964), p.21.
4. Virginia Satir, *Peoplemaking* (Science and Behavior Books, 1972), p.125.

6 Sex within Marriage

Is it wrong to go into marriage with high expectations of the sexual relationship? In the last chapter we acknowledged that this was not wrong. On the contrary, 'sensitive, effective and satisfying sex forms the heart of wholesome marriages'. Is this an extravagant claim?

An accurate understanding of the many meanings of sexual intercourse within marriage affirms it. The value of wholesome sex within marriage must not be underestimated, neither, of course, must it be over-glamorized.

Sexual intercourse is a magnificent act. Part of its grandeur rests in one of its functions; it enables two people to share with God in the creation of new life. 'With the help of the Lord I have brought forth a man' (Gn. 4:1). This is awesome. It fulfils a command of God (Gn. 1:28). Procreation, giving birth to a child, is one of the purposes of sex. It receives much praise in the Old Testament (Ps. 127:3–5; Pr. 17:6) and it should be regarded as one of the chief privileges of marriage. But procreation is not the only function of marital union. Since procreation is possible only during a limited period of the woman's monthly cycle, and since the longevity of her reproductive life is restricted, intercourse clearly has other purposes. In fact in these days of reliable contraception, over 90% of sexual intercourse in marriage will not be for the intention of procreation. Rather, the intention will be for pleasure. Did God envisage people enjoying sex? Genesis 2:24 finds God giving clear instructions to the couple which will safeguard their sexual and emotional unity. 'For this reason a man will leave his father and mother and be united to his wife, and they will become one flesh.' This sexual unity left the couple without shame.

The Bible's view of sex is positive and accepting. In God's

own reported words, He saw all that He had made, including the genitalia of the male and female, and He saw that it was 'very good' (Gn. 1:31). Thus the sexual dimension of marriage is not merely approved by God; it finds its origin in Him.

Unfortunately the early Fathers of the Christian church misconstrued the meanings of sex, even within marriage. Their warped teaching distorted the beauty of intercourse and made it ugly. Misinformed Christians became bewildered. This confusion between church teaching and biblical teaching reverberated down the centuries and its echoes do not die. They seek an answering call from Christian couples today. But we owe it to one another not to approach marriage befuddled by misconceptions which disguise the true meaning of sex within marriage. For this reason, an attempt to disentangle the erroneous teaching of the early Fathers from biblical teaching must be made.

The teaching of the church

After Paul's lofty description of marriage in Ephesians 5, an air of negativism pervaded the church's teaching on marriage. Thus Gregory of Nyssa, whose teaching was acclaimed at the Council of Constantinople in AD 381, dismissed marriage as a 'sad tragedy'. He concluded that Adam and Eve could not have had sexual relations in their pre-fallen state. His dogmatic pronouncement, 'there would never have been such an institution were it not for original sin',[1] influenced successive teaching, particularly Augustine's.

This pessimistic view of marriage was adopted by John Chrysostom, Bishop of Constantinople, who subscribed to the belief that marriage hindered the greatest possible service to God. He reasoned that there would have been no need for sexual intercourse if Adam had not fallen into disobedience.

Although these views find no support in the Bible, they were taken up by Ambrose, who condemned marriage as a 'galling burden'. Even St Augustine perpetuated the claim that marriage is a blighted relationship. To his credit, he dismissed the idea that marriage was a result of original sin, but he put forward the view that the first sin of Adam and Eve was a sexual one. He therefore reached the unfortunate conclusion that the sexual act transmits original sin. In fact he claimed that intercourse is always accompanied by sin. This sinful element is removed only if intercourse is performed solely for the purpose of creating new life, procreation.

Gregory I went further. Although he conceded that intercourse was, of itself, not sinful, the pleasure attached to it was wrong. Since couples could not avoid the pleasurable element even when they did desire to create new life, the sex act was condemned. Couples were instructed to abstain from intercourse before receiving Communion and while preparing for baptism. He further degraded sex by implying that, even within marriage, it was dirty. Hence men should not enter church after indulging in intercourse unless they had washed first. Arnobius, too, felt coitus was filthy.

As Jack Dominian shows in his fascinating survey of this early church teaching, the links with the positive approach of the Old and New Testaments were severed. Healthy biblical teaching was overlaid by a 'wealth of adverse remarks', austerity and severity of thinking.

For Catholics, the wind of change was felt when Abelard insisted that intercourse itself *and* the pleasure which accompanies it are both good. They are good because they originate in God. In the thirteenth century, William of Auvergne admitted that 'Intercourse...can involve a spiritual pleasure'. By the seventeenth century, Francis de Sales pierced the gloom with his revolutionary teaching: 'Marital intercourse is certainly holy, lawful and praiseworthy in itself and profitable to society.'[2] Gradually Catholics emerged from the sludge of narrow, constricting beliefs. The procreative and unitive purposes of sex within marriage were both recognized. Sexual relations were seen to be fulfilling.

Meanwhile the Protestant revolution of the sixteenth century opposed the error in the church's teaching. As Luther expressed it: 'Marriage consists of these things; the natural desire of sex, the bringing to life of offspring, and life together with mutual fidelity.'[3]

He went further. His denunciation of clerical hypocrisy was brutal:

The pope and his cardinals, monks, nuns and priests have tried to improve things and ordain a holy estate in which they might live in holiness and chastity. But how holy, pure and chaste [their] lives...have been is so apparent that the sun, moon and stars have cried out against it.... Why, then, did this happen? Because they tore down and despised God's holy ordinance of the estate of matrimony and they were not worthy to enter into marriage.[4]

And so the climate changed. The biting wind of asceticism gave way to the warmth of biblical teaching. Married couples became free to enjoy sexual intercourse and the accompanying pleasures were recognized as part of God's design. Recent insights highlight the wonder of this gift from God. Unfortunately, although the church's teaching is now generally in alignment with the Bible's, confusion lingers.

What are your feelings about sexual intercourse?

Maybe you feel that couples should blush when they reflect on the sexual enjoyment marriage offers?

If these are your feelings, acknowledge them. But at the same time bring biblical truth alongside these erroneous ideas.

The teaching of the Bible

Adam seems to have known nothing of the pessimism we have studied. In the presence of his sexual partner, it was as if he burst into song (Gn. 2:23).

Love prompts another ecstatic outburst in the Song of Solomon. This love-poem implies that, far from being dirty, degraded and shameful, sex is the means of leading each partner into transports of delight. It is a language with more dimensions than words. This language conveys a dynamic message. It is the certainty of joyful abandonment to one another, passionate oneness with each other and an enduring acceptance of the other.

These unspoken joys are wholly satisfying in a permanent relationship. At least, the writer of Proverbs encourages us in this belief. 'May you rejoice in the wife of your youth....may her breasts satisfy you always, may you ever be captivated by her love' (Pr. 5:18–19).

The New Testament takes up this joyous theme and develops it. For Paul, marriage, with its emphasis on regular sexual involvement (1 Cor. 7:5), reflects the union that exists between Christ and the church. It is a mystery; but this glorious mystery must be contained within the marital relationship. How else can it mirror and represent the permanence of the love Christ pours out on His bride? It is only within marriage, that relationship which reflects the relational dimension of the Trinity, that a couple can plumb the depths of this act. Remove intercourse from marriage and you mock at the mystery which we only partially understand.

The significance of sexual intercourse

Sexual intercourse is body language. It sometimes makes use of words, but it has no need of them. Sexual intimacy communicates its unique messages wordlessly. What are these messages?

Sexual fusion says, 'I want you.' That message cures loneliness. A lonely person is one who is independent, who has found no secure place of belonging. To find that security in the intimacy of the body of one who loves you brings peace.

This sense of well-being confirms our acceptability. This reassurance provides an answer to that searching question, 'Who am I?' As Jack Dominian puts it:

> In the sexual act there is in the physical and emotional closeness a recurrent confirmation on the part of the spouses that each matters sufficiently to the other to be accepted as a whole person, with his or her physical strength and limitations, mental achievements and failures, emotional fears and anxieties.[5]

Each partner affirms the other sexually; a sexual celebration takes place.

This celebration revels in the trust, loyalty and confidence the spouses have for each other. They each rejoice in the assurance that one person in this world is 'all for me'. And this certainty eliminates the fear of rejection, dispels the fear of betrayal and heals the pain of abandonment. Satisfactory sex within marriage safeguards couples from the crippling pain of isolation.

Satisfying sex also strengthens a marital relationship. When two married people bring one another to sexual orgasm, they communicate the non-verbal message, 'You are both loved and lovable.' This is the message every person needs to hear. This blissful certainty is accompanied by another. Satisfying sex gives each partner a sense of achievement.

Sensitive sexual relating in marriage is wordless affirmation of the other: 'You are the most precious person in my life.' It conveys the silent message of gratitude, 'Thank you for being there'; of hope, 'I hope you will be here tomorrow' and of completion, 'I discover myself completely when I am fused with you.'

This mystery, this 'one flesh' relationship, therefore offers many of the conditions necessary for emotional maturity. Acceptance, trust, achievement and affirmation produce whole people. And zestful sex produces another by-product. It is the place where reconciliation for quarrels and disagreements are found. Sexual oneness transcends differences. That is not to say that differences of opinion are automatically resolved when two people make love. Any conflict in the marriage must still be worked through with patience and forgiveness. But when couples enjoy sexual intimacy, they become highly motivated to preserve the total unity of the marriage. In that sense, sexual oneness transcends differences and provides a couple with the determination to continue to work at the relationship.

As Paul implies, when two people make love, something deep and irrevocable happens (see 1 Cor. 6:12–20). That is why this physical celebration should be reserved for marriage. When they come together sexually, two people fuse to become one. Robin Skynner puts it well:

In a fulfilling sexual act, the two opposite genders, at their most different and separate, simultaneously become one totally, merging with one another in an experience going beyond the capacity of either. Each is most centred in, and aware of, himself or herself, yet also wholly open and responsive to the other. Each temporarily loses his boundary, surrenders to a greater unity. Both are as spontaneous as they could ever be, yet this spontaneity is possible because of a fundamental self-discipline, an ability to deny oneself, to wait, to adapt and adjust to the other as in the unfolding of a dance. It is non-manipulative, non-controlling; the self is offered freely, from generosity and trust, and since there is no demand the return comes equally freely and fully, each emotionally responding and keeping time with the other, each gives most generously yet takes most uninhibitedly too, without hedging or bargaining....And the climax, when it 'comes' in its own time, is productive, creative, sometimes through the beginning of a separate new life but always in a renewal of the separate lives of the partners and the joint life of their relationship, so that the wild, single act of affirmation is never tired of, never loses its fullness or the refreshing quality of a draught of spring water or mountain air.[6]

The good news about sex within marriage is that it is not a guilty secret. On the contrary, sexual pleasure between husband and wife is a part of the wonder of God's creation. It is a language through which couples communicate a variety of messages which rise from the depths of the inner self. With God, therefore, married couples may rejoice in this renewable refreshment. It is 'very good'. It is so very good that it is worth waiting for. Unwrap this gift prematurely and you strip it of many of its unexpected delights. For intercourse is a magnificent act: but it is for marriage.

Notes for chapter six

1. Quoted by Jack Dominian, *Christian Marriage* (Libra, 1977), p.26.
2. *Christian Marriage*, pp.55f.
3. Quoted by Julia O'Faolain and Lauro Martines (eds.), *Not in God's Image* (Fontana, 1974), p.209.
4. *Not in God's Image*, p.210.
5. *Christian Marriage*, p.113.
6. Robin Skynner, *One Flesh: Separate Persons* (Constable, 1976), p.129.

7 Sex before Marriage

In the last chapter we observed that sex *within* marriage is a magnificent act; that the sexual activity of marriage delights God; that the Bible's view of marital sex is positive, accepting and attractive.

But where does sex *before* marriage fit in? Pam felt confused about this when she started at university. She's attractive, and young men invited her out. She soon discovered that most of them expected intercourse in exchange for a coffee date. But Pam is a Christian. She doesn't believe in casual sleeping around and she felt isolated and lonely. Was she wrong to stick to her Christian principles? How long can she cope with being the only girl on her corridor who isn't sleeping with her boy-friend? What will happen when she finds herself overwhelmed by sexual desire?

Some student nurses known to us found themselves equally bewildered. Most of their colleagues, too, paired off and slept together. Some lived together. Should these Christians similarly indulge in free sex? Some did and they felt guilty. Others abstained and exposed themselves to cruel jibes. 'You Christians are wet.' 'Are you gay?'

Such taunts sting. This hurt prompted them to organize a seminar in which they invited us to examine these pressing questions. 'Is sex before marriage all right? If not, what biblical teaching is there? Is there anything wrong with sleeping around?'

In this chapter, I plan to answer those questions and to look at another. Does the Bible say anything about sex for the engaged couple?

I sometimes find myself hurting inside when I talk to young people oppressed by these problems. I am well aware that Christians are as sexually alive as their unbelieving friends; that coping with powerful waves of sexual desire is hard, seemingly impossible; that the frustration sometimes seems intolerable. These reflections on the Bible's teaching and observations from counselling experience may seem like mere headlamps in the fog. Perhaps they will offer a glimmer of light, a degree of protection?

What does the Bible say about sex, unfaithfulness and casual sex?

As we have seen, the Bible finds no problem with zestful sexual activity when the context is marriage. Take Genesis 2:24–25, for example. When a man leaves his father and mother and commits himself to his wife, the assumption is that they will become one flesh.

Or take Proverbs 5:18–19. 'So be happy with...the girl you married...Let her charms keep you happy; let her surround you with her love' (GNB). Satisfying sex and marriage are happy bedfellows. Paul underlines this biblical principle. When he addresses the promiscuous Corinthians, he does not disallow sexual pleasure but he does place it in context: 'Let each man have his own wife and each woman her own husband' (1 Cor. 7:2 JB). The implication is that within the bond of marriage sex is permitted, indeed expected and encouraged.

Why this emphasis on marriage? Paul gives the answer to that question in Ephesians 5:32, where he suggests that this mysterious fusion of two persons is intended to reflect the permanence of the union which exists between Christ and His bride, the church. Contemporary observations about the sex act seem to be saying something similar. It is now widely acknowledged that sexual intercourse between married partners transforms the individuality of the man and the woman. It welds the 'I' and the 'thou' into a new entity, the 'we', without cancelling out the 'I' or the 'thou'.

This unitive act is a pale reflection of the oneness which has always existed between the three members of the Trinity and which exists between Christ and the church.

If this is true, if this merging of two bodies symbolizes such permanence and depth, what happens when people sleep around, when married persons commit adultery?

In 1 Corinthians 6:13ff. Paul explains what happens to the Christian who prostitutes his/her body in extra-marital sexual activity. This person dishonours his/her own body, violates the sex act itself and defiles God's property. Sexual immorality is seen as a serious transgression.

> The body is not meant for sexual immorality, but for the Lord, and the Lord for the body. By his power God raised the Lord from the dead, and he will raise us also. Do you not know that your bodies are members of Christ himself? Shall I then take the members of Christ and unite them with a prostitute? Never! Do you not know that he who unites himself with a prostitute is one with her in body? For it is said, 'The two will become one flesh.' But he who unites himself with the Lord is one with him in spirit.
> Flee from sexual immorality. All other sins a man commits are outside his body, but he who sins sexually sins against his own body. Do you not know that your body is a temple of the Holy Spirit, who is in you, whom you have received from God? You are not your own; you were bought at a price. Therefore honour God with your body.
>
> (1 Cor. 6:13–20)

How does sleeping around degrade your own body? It insults your body because you are not a toy, a thing to be used, played with and discarded. Your body is a part of the glory of God's creation, stamped with His hallmark, with dignity and honour. Moreover, your body is a temple of the Holy Spirit, the place where Jesus resides, which is sacred for His use (v. 19). Can a Christian therefore contemplate involving the indwelling Spirit in a disposable, incomplete, shallow sexual relationship? Isn't it unthinkable?

It is unthinkable until you find yourself powerfully drawn to a person of the opposite sex. Then what? What if the desire to give your body to another is strong? Paul's response to that problem is the reminder that 'You are not your own property; you have been bought and paid for' (v. 20 JB). Our bodies are not ours to prostitute. They have been purchased by Christ's sacrifice on Calvary. For what purpose? 'God did not call us to live in immorality, but in holiness' (1 Thes. 4:7 GNB). When you are tempted to sleep with your partner before you are married, will you remind yourself that to do so would be to defile your body, God's property; to act contrary to God's love?

Sexual intercourse seals the permanent union contracted between husband and wife. It illustrates, in a physical, biological way, the unity to which they have committed themselves socially, spiritually, emotionally, in relationship to one another and the community. It is also symbolic of the eternal union which exists between Christ and the church. Are you prepared to mock this rich symbolism by indulging in the one-night stand, casual sex, intercourse as a thank-you for a happy evening? You may try, but if you do you attempt the impossible.

As Paul emphasizes in 1 Corinthians 6:15, sexual intercourse unites persons in a deep, inextricable, irrevocable union. There is, therefore, no such thing as casual sex. Even if you 'use' a prostitute, you become one with her.

These are hard sayings for Christians living in the West today. They were hard, too, for converts living in Corinth and Thessalonica in the first century. How were they to move into a new gear when all around them promiscuity was accepted as a normal way of life? Aware that sexual immorality incurred the wrath of God (1 Thes. 4:6), they refused to take their standards from contemporary society. They knew that sexual vice was to be shunned (1 Thes. 4:3; 1 Cor. 6:18); that they could be free from sexploitation (1 Thes. 4:6); that they must pursue a higher calling: to love and to serve. Did this come easily? I doubt it. Freedom from slavery to sex rarely does. Do you want to base *your* code of behaviour on society's clamour for free sex or on the Bible's teaching? Will you keep sexual activity for marriage? Will you control the sexual side of your relationship in order to bring pleasure to God? (See 1 Thes. 4:6.)

Where will you erect your boundaries?

Paul and Wendy really wanted to enjoy sex within the security of marriage. But they were medical students. After they'd been going out together for two years they got engaged.

They looked forward to marriage with eagerness. Then Wendy's parents withheld their permission to allow Wendy to marry until both she and Paul had qualified. They would be engaged for another three years.

Paul and Wendy already felt that they had been growing in their commitment to each other. They felt deeply united in spirit, soul, mind, emotions. Why not become sexually one, then? Surely God was not so black and white that He would expect them to wait? Surely they were not sinning? They were deeply in love, sincere in their commitment and could not be accused of behaving promiscuously.

Does the Bible say anything about sex for the engaged couple?

The honest answer is 'No!'. The Bible has no word for engagement as we know it today. The nearest parallel is betrothal. But betrothal was a far more binding contract than engagement. Matthew 1:18 illustrates this, where we read of Joseph planning to 'divorce' Mary. To back out of the commitment of betrothal was as complicated as divorce used to be in this country.

So how does the Bible view sex for betrothed couples? It still demands virginity. Take Deuteronomy 22:13–21. This passage describes what sometimes happened to a bride on her wedding-night. She was compelled to prove her virginity. If she could not do this, her husband acted within his legal rights if he chose to divorce her forthwith. Or take Matthew 1:18–19. The secrecy, shame and embarrassment with which Mary's pre-marital pregnancy was handled surely point to the same fact. Sex before marriage, even between couples who were legally committed to one another in betrothal, was illicit. Sex is for marriage.

Jewish custom seemed to have exercised strict control over women, while ignoring male promiscuity. But this sexual licence was ruled out of court when the Christian church formed its own moral code of behaviour. As early as Acts 15:20, we find James writing to new converts forbidding any indulgence in sexual immorality.

Jesus Himself encourages us to think seriously about our

sexual activity. He condemns adultery, and warns against the unfaithfulness which expresses itself in subtle ways. 'Anyone who looks at a woman and wants to possess her is guilty of committing adultery with her' (Mt. 5:28 GNB). It was not that Jesus was an antisexual ascetic. If this were true He would not have reiterated God's creation plan. 'Haven't you read...that at the beginning the Creator "made them male and female", and said, "For this reason a man will leave his father and mother and be united to his wife, and the two will become one flesh"? So they are no longer two, but one' (Mt. 19:4–6). Clearly Jesus approved of sexual fusion when the context was marriage.

How are you feeling about Jesus' standards?

The Bible, in my opinion, leaves us in no doubt that the gem of intercourse has one setting, marriage. It implies that if you remove sex from marriage you distort both the act and the relationship. It nowhere gives even a hint of a clause permitting sex outside the marital relationship. Why?

Why keep sex within marriage?

Isn't it unreasonable to ask a couple like Paul and Wendy to wait for three years before they can enjoy sexual oneness? Yes, it is unreasonable. I ached for them when they came to talk to me. But this unreasonableness must be laid at the parents' feet, I feel, not God's. Society is quick to blame God, quick to turn the God of love into a tyrant. This tendency is not new. It first appears in Genesis 3:1. 'Did God really say...?' How unreasonable! We sin most easily when we are tempted to believe an exaggerated view of God's harshness which Satan, the world, or our own rebellious feelings whisper to us. But those of us involved in the caring ministry, who see the casualties extra-marital sex produces, know the subtle injury which the act often inflicts. We see the wounds, sometimes deep, often permanent. To us it is more clear why God circumscribes our journey through life with rules. They are for our protection. As one man put it to me once, 'Starting from the reality of my pain it became clear that God's law was not an arbitrary imposition, but, like all good laws, a protection against the inevitable consequences of crime –

hurt, division, betrayal. Faced with this overwhelming desire to sleep with Joan, I suddenly saw that law is a loving thing. God's law is eminently sensible. It prevents people getting hurt.'

If you've heard someone admit, 'I just cannot forgive myself. I can't forget,' you will know how crippling a guilt-ridden memory can be. This guilt separates a person from God. It then turns to fear, anger or anxiety. It sometimes develops physical symptoms, but more frequently results in depression. Of course, I am not saying that all persons who indulge in pre-marital sex will automatically nose-dive into depression later in life. I am saying that it is a common phenomenon. God wants to protect us from this emotional pain. Will you place yourself under His protection?

God also wants couples to enjoy sexual activity when they are married. It frequently happens that those couples who enjoy sexual experimentation before they are married, lose interest in the sexual relationship after they have been married for a few years. Again, this does not always happen, but it occurs frequently. As one woman put it, describing her pre-marital sexual experience, 'It was all so furtive. I hated it.' This hatred spilt over into her marriage after her children were born. Her husband feels cheated. God would save us from this ruination of sexual pleasure.

And He longs to rescue Karen from the frigidity which is the physical handicap pre-marital sex left her with. Before Karen and Graham married, they enjoyed sex. Graham brought Karen to orgasm frequently. But now frozen guilt holds Karen in its grip. Disappointing sex spoils their relationship.

It seems, then, that Walter Trobisch is right. Pre-marital sex is rather like picking blossom in spring. It seems beautiful, right and natural at the time. But when autumn comes, there is no fruit. Sexual pleasure in marriage should become better and better. God longs to prevent us from spoiling that wonderful prospect.

I am aware that, for every reader who has experimented with pre-marital sex and suffered the pain, disillusionment and dismay I have described, there will be another who was not left feeling empty, disappointed or isolated. Some people behave promiscuously and appear to bear few lasting scars. Does that make sex outside marriage right? I don't think so.

Responsible love

Sex, as we have seen, belongs in the context of committed love. This love involves a permanent commitment to the well-being of the loved one. As John Powell reminds us, 'Love rejects the question "What am I getting out of this?"'[1] In fact, 'Love immediately challenges me to break the fixation I have with myself....Love demands that I learn how to focus my attention on the needs of those I love.'[2] Or as the Bible puts it, 'You must love...your neighbour as yourself' (Lk. 10:27 JB).

People who love themselves accept responsibility for themselves: they avoid unnecessary pain or needless injury. So they pull their hand out of the flame or jump out of reach of an oncoming bus. If you love yourself as God loves you, therefore, you have to enquire, before indulging in extra-marital sex, 'Will I get hurt?' Supposing a child is accidentally conceived? Supposing I catch V.D.? Supposing this act, which is so much more than the mere biological joining of two bodies, unleashes dependency feelings in me which I didn't know existed, which I can't control? After all, two people who fuse their bodies with abandonment and trust cannot expect to be the same afterwards. They are one flesh. Sex is the language of intimacy, of commitment, of passion. It affects, not just my body, but the whole of me. Am I likely to get hurt if I sleep with my partner? How do I feel about confiscating my wholeness which Christ died to secure?

'You must love...your neighbour as yourself.' If this is true, you will have to ask yourself these questions:

What is this extra-marital sex act going to do for your partner? Will he/she be hurt?

To love is to bear responsibility for the loved one. Supposing a child is accidentally conceived? How will your partner feel? How would the unwanted child feel?

If you sleep together now, how will it affect your partner's view of himself/herself? How will it affect his/her future?

How will the memories further marital happiness? Might they destroy it?

Will sleeping together deepen your partner's relationship with God or ruin it?

Will it enhance his/her view of sex, God's symbol of permanent love, or cheapen it?

Are you using your partner's body to give you quick thrills? Is that love or the abuse of love? Do you really want to trivialize sex and your partner?

How do you feel about engaging in pre-marital sex with your partner? How do you feel about discussing these questions with him/her?

If you decide that the world's standard, sexual licence, is not compatible with the Bible's standard, you must ask another question: how will we abstain?

Anyone who claims that this is easy is not speaking the truth. It is difficult, but not impossible.

Sex is a hunger. It clamours to be fed on demand. Shall we then be manipulated by screaming feelings? Sexual feelings are like petulant children. Does a wise mother always give in to her child's demands? Loving parents learn when to refuse a request, when to say 'Wait'. Likewise, as adults, we must learn to discipline our rebel emotions.

Discipline

Discipline? Isn't this harmful? No! Discipline is not harmful. It is not the same as repression. Repression harms people because it means pushing feelings firmly into the subconscious, then living as though the feelings do not exist. This pretence is short-lived. These feelings will spring out again, but in a disguised form. Clearly repression is unhealthy.

Discipline, on the other hand, never involves sweeping feelings into a dark corner. Discipline is seen when the understanding adult listens to the complaints of unhappy children, interprets them accurately and meets the real rather than the expressed needs. In other words, when you and your partner discipline yourselves, you listen to your own feelings with sensitivity but you do not give in to every desire. That is a travesty of love, not its full expression.

This discipline need not be mournful. It can be exciting, like deciding not to peep inside parcels until Christmas Day.

This discipline is healthy, joyful, balanced. It adds dignity to yourself, your partner and your sexuality. You are no longer enslaved by sexual desire. You control it.

God does not ask you to control it alone. He gives the Holy Spirit to strengthen our moral fibre when resolve is weak. I think this is what Paul implies in 1 Thessalonians 4:8. It is only the indwelling Spirit of Jesus who enables us to walk unscathed through the heat of passionate desire. He is the one who cultivates the patience we need to receive God's gifts in God's time, including the gift of sexual fulfilment in marriage. He is the one who produces the self-control which dogged determination on its own fails to produce. And He is the one who causes the fruit of gentleness, kindness and responsible love to grow within us; those qualities which refuse us permission to abuse our own body or the body of another. When the strength of sexual desire renders us helpless, it casts us back on God's unfailing help. Then in our weakness we become strong. For discipline shot through by the grace of God results in joyful obedience, in sexual battles won.

For thirty years Augustine refused to avail himself of this supernatural help. Then he had an encounter with God. Reflecting on his life of promiscuity he lamented this dead-end seeking in this way, 'Too late have I loved you, O Lord, too late have I loved you. Memory is indeed a sad privilege.'

What sacrifices are you prepared to make to ensure that you master sex rather than allowing sex to master you?

In chapter 9 we return to this subject and consider how to express affection responsibly. But maybe you feel daunted by what I have just written? What if it is too late, if you have already indulged in extra-marital sex? Have you committed the unforgivable sin? Of course not. The next chapter spells out the good news. In Christ lost virginity can be restored.

Notes for chapter seven

1. John Powell, *Unconditional Love* (Argus, 1978), p.56.
2. *Unconditional Love*, p.88.

8 Treating the Indelible Stain

Pre-marital experimentation leaves its mark, as we saw in the last chapter. Is this stain indelible, one which cannot be erased? The Bible encourages us in the belief that sexual sin, like any other, can be washed clean by the forgiveness of Christ. That does not mean we are at liberty to sin because forgiveness is readily available. That is cheap grace. But you pay a high price for it! As one man put it to me once, 'It's hard to forget the past even when you know you are forgiven.' Reflecting on his own promiscuous past, he asked this question, 'What was it about Jesus that made His ministry so effective? What did He do for Mary Magdalene which restored her so completely?'

Jesus' ministry to a promiscuous and adulterous generation was authoritative, powerful and full of compassion. Take the woman caught committing adultery, for example. He seems to have accurately understood her feelings, her despair. His ministry was fourfold. He forgave, He healed, He released and He re-established her.

As we shall go on to see in this chapter, when Jesus forgives, He gives a person a new start. His forgiveness is accompanied by unconditional acceptance of the sinner. This is healing. Of course, Jesus never condones sin, but He does love sinners. He is able to cut them free from the failure which so often seems like an entangled mesh strangling every attempt to move. When He sets people free from the past, He sets them free to a life of usefulness once more.

Is this ministry still available today? I believe it is. Through the ministry of prayer it is still possible for a person who has transgressed God's moral law to be restored. The result? It is exactly as if they were virgins again.

Do you want to avail yourself of this ministry which the

Lord offers so freely? Of course, this will not encourage the Christian to indulge in sexual sin because forgiveness is easy (Rom. 6:1).

I repeat, I am not talking about cheap grace. I am reminding Christians that the forgiveness of God is freely available. Anyone, therefore, who knows about forgiveness but who has never applied this healing balm to the open sores of the past may be reassured. Sexual sin is not the unforgivable sin. On the contrary, God delights to pour the ointment of forgiveness into the stench of the wounds we examined in the last chapter. This is the good news the Bible proclaims, 'Lord, if you keep in mind our sins then who can ever get an answer to his prayers? But you forgive! What an awesome thing this is!' (Ps. 130:3–4 LB).

Jim discovered this truth for himself when he turned to Christ. He knew that his failure was punishable, that he deserved God's anger. He was ashamed. So when he heard that, although he was guilty, Christ loved him enough to wipe the slate clean, he repented, turned his back on the past, and accepted the forgiveness so freely offered by the Lord. Like a condemned criminal released from his sentence, Jim rejoiced.

He turned his back on the past in repentance. This step is vital, as Tom is discovering. Like Jim, he also experienced the deep cleansing of the blood of Christ which sealed off a promiscuous past. But Tom has not repented. He still proudly cherishes the memories of the sexual conquests he made in the past. Until he allows God to transform his attitudes, the work of forgiveness will remain incomplete.

The healing touch of Christ
Jim discovered the refreshment of God's forgiveness after he had fallen into sexual sin. Is there forgiveness for the Christian who deliberately disobeys God? I believe there is (1 Jn. 1:9). Never allow Satan to whisper the lie that God has abandoned you because of your disobedience. This is a distortion of the truth. Sin does make God angry. But, as Jonah reminds us, He is 'a gracious God, merciful, slow to get angry, and full of kindness' (Jon. 4:2 LB). Or as Jesus reminds us through the

parable of the returning son, as soon as the Father sees the stirrings of repentance in our hearts, He runs to greet us, to welcome, restore and forgive us (Lk. 15).

Christine knew this in her head. She had heard this teaching from infancy. But when she had slept around at college with single students and with a married man, her own heart condemned her. She could not receive the free forgiveness God offered, until the day she confessed her sin to another Christian. When this counsellor reminded her of the words of Jesus to the woman caught sleeping with a married man, 'Neither do I [condemn you]. Go and sin no more' (Jn 8:11 LB), Christine wept. And gradually the all-too-familiar cross of our Lord took on new meaning. As she knelt at the foot of that cross, and imagined the body of the Lord writhing in pain, she knew that He was strung out there, not just for the whole world, but for her. And she wept again, tears of sorrow mingled with joy, tears of cleansing.

Jesus forgave. He still forgives. He will go on forgiving. John also understood those words. After all, he was a preacher. But this message of cleansing did not flow from his head to his heart until he opened himself to the healing touch of Christ. John's work took him to a lonely outback. There the aloneness of the ministry overwhelmed him. He found solace in the arms of a married woman, and slept with her. His Christian usefulness was finished, or so he thought. What was it that released Mary Magdalene from the bondage of this kind of guilt and sin? Was it the words of Jesus? Or was it the non-verbal communication: the acceptance she read in His eyes, the love she saw on His face, the affirmation she detected in His touch? The Gospel narrative remains silent in answer to this question. I believe it must have been both. And through prayer, God seemed to give John access to both kinds of communication.

I prayed with John and we returned in imagination to the place where he had disobeyed God. Where was Jesus? What was He thinking, doing, feeling about John? As we prayed, God seemed to touch John's memory so that he could recall the incident in vivid detail. But this time, the re-play included not just John and the woman. Jesus was also there. John could see Him: Jesus had been there in the room with them all the time. John, too, had been caught in the act of adultery. But those eyes of Jesus spoke, not of condemnation, but of love. The face expressed, not rejection, but forgiveness. And the voice seemed to say, 'Neither do I condemn you. Go and sin no more.' When John confessed this time, he was not grovelling. On the contrary, he was pouring out the anguish, not of one moment, but of years. But he was ready now to open his clenched fists to receive the forgiveness which before had been theory but which now became therapy. This forgiveness had been applied by God to the place which stung. It brought healing and release. And this reassurance restored John again, not just to the Lord, but to himself in self-acceptance and to society in usefulness. Jesus *is* able to remove the sting from painful memories so that ghosts of the past cease to hold you in their grip. The past which is opened to Jesus no longer holds the present in a paralysis.

Did you squirm as you read chapter 7? Do *you* need to open yourself to the kind of ministry described above? I am not suggesting that you reduce the person of Jesus to aspirin proportions. I am not saying, 'Take this pill and all will be well.' I am saying that Jesus longs to set you free from the past. 'So if the Son sets you free, you will be free indeed' (Jn. 8:36).

Why, then, do some Christians remain in bondage to the past? Why are some restored instantly through prayer while others seem unable to free themselves from the tentacles of sin and hurt which hold them in their grip?

I know no slick answer to these questions and there is no point in 'playing God' and pretending that the questions have easy answers. Healing, forgiveness, release and restoration are gifts from God. They are His to give as and when He chooses.

Some people come for the kind of prayer ministry I have described apparently prepared by God to enter into the joy of wholeness and release immediately. It all seems so easy. Others come equally expectant that God can and will work but He seems to entrust them with the more difficult task of growing into wholeness one step at a time. Perhaps this is because He has many lessons to teach them in the growing process. Maybe He knows that they could not live with a sudden reversal of circumstances but they can cope with the slow process of gradual healing. And who is to say which is the more powerful? Our eyes must always be on the giver, God, and not on the way He chooses to deliver His people. But, of course, if you come to God to ask for forgiveness, you must also be prepared to forgive yourself. It is not permissible for us as Christians so to magnify our sinfulness that we minimize the grace of God. And if you really want the kind of healing I have described, you have to be prepared to walk away from the past with its sin and its pain. In other words, you have to be prepared to move into partnership with God and to grow up as a person and this maturing is not without cost to yourself. But isn't this what Jesus was implying when He said to the woman caught in the act of adultery, 'Go and sin no more' (Jn. 8:11)?

The pain of our partner's failures
The thing that troubled Geoff was not his own lost virginity. That was intact. But Caroline, his wife, had slept with a previous partner. Although Geoff wanted to forgive her, he found he could not do it. This lack of forgiveness frightened him and made inroads into their sexual relationship. He frequently felt that Caroline compared his sexual 'performance' unfavourably with that of 'this other guy'. This made Geoff feel insecure and this anxiety had penetrating roots. On the day Caroline had broken the news to Geoff, he had felt betrayed. Could he trust her? Did he still love her? He did and so they married. But he had never faced the initial shock *with Christ*. He had failed to ask the vital question, 'How does the Lord feel about her?' We prayed together therefore and we returned to that grassy bank where Geoff first heard Caroline blurt out that she was not a virgin. In prayer, we asked the Lord to make it clear how He felt about Caroline, about Geoff, about their relationship. It was then that Geoff understood, with the heart and with the mind, that when Caroline confessed to God, He had blotted out her failure. In God's sight she was clean. This realization set Geoff free to

forgive her too. This forgiveness did not erase the old memories, but it removed the sting from those memories. Geoff and Caroline did not play 'Let's pretend' – 'Let's pretend it never happened.' Rather, they acknowledged just what did happen. They placed the past into the arms of Christ and walked resolutely away from it. This is healing, reconciliation and growth. It enabled them to enjoy years of satisfying marital sex and to accept one another more fully.

Victims of sexual abuse

This good news, that Jesus' ministry is as effective today as when He walked this earth, stunned Sheila. She feared that she would never marry. She hated any kind of physical closeness and felt that love-making even in marriage would be intolerable. When she was twelve, Sheila had been the victim of attempted rape. Since then, her distrust of men, of touch and of sex had become a part of life, like washing up the breakfast things. Could God break into this situation? He did. For Sheila, there was no re-living of the past. That would have been too painful. It was enough for her to receive the ministry of the laying-on-of-hands and prayer. By means of this prayer, the Lord set her free from the fears of the past and she is now happily married.

I think of another girl, Jenny. She suffered greatly from the early memory of discovering her mother making love to her god-father. After that, Jenny could not bear to watch love-scenes on the television or in films. If she stumbled on a couple kissing on a park bench, she fled. It was when she availed herself of specific prayer for this situation that God set her free from paralysing attitudes. She forgave her mother for one thing, and she is now able to watch love-scenes without panic. She is also learning to give and receive love with greater freedom. The memories are not erased, but they have lost their sting.

Why have I introduced so many damaged people into this chapter? If you did not find yourself in the pages of chapter 7, you may well be asking this question. But if you have suffered, or still hurt as a result of extra-marital sex, you will under-stand why this chapter is essential to this book. Or it may be that your sexual wrong turning involved homosexual or perverted practices. The same forgiveness and healing are available. The Lord is able to purge the sins of the past, whatever you have done. He is able to bring you into wholeness even though the way back may be an uphill struggle.

When Jesus met the woman at the well (Jn. 4), He brought her face to face with her problem; adultery. It hurt. She wriggled, but she believed. 'Come and see a man who has told me everything I ever did; I wonder if he is the Christ?' (v. 29 JB).

Reassurance

I believe there is a spiritual principle here. Jesus wants us to give Him access to everything we have ever done, including our sexual misdemeanours, including the memories which haunt us because we have been hurt by others. When the light of His presence pervades this darkness, it transforms. We can never claim, 'It didn't happen.' That would be less than honest. What we can claim is, 'It happened to me and the Lord saw, loved and forgave.' That assurance brings healing.

People often ask me why specific prayer is necessary. Why do we need the laying-on-of-hands? Surely blanket forgiveness is enough? There is a sense in which *the fact* that Christ died for you is enough. For some people it clearly is, like Jim whom I mentioned at the beginning of this chapter.

But others seem to need more intimate reassurance. God, in His love and desire for our wholeness, does not withhold that reassurance. Just as He sent Ananias to minister to Paul (Acts 9:17), so He touches us through one another. It is a mystery.

We should not despise those who need specific help for particular needs. No-one can really understand the trauma another person may have experienced through sexual indulgence or assault. We must not criticize. Rather, we must rejoice that God understands, cares and heals. He is like a nurse skilfully anointing the running sores of our lives with water and ointment and love. He is not careless with His nursing, so He does not throw the ointment over us in a hit-and-miss fashion. Each sore which eats at our flesh matters to Him and can be treated by Him. When you receive this healing, you awaken to the realization that salvation (wholeness) covers not just the sins of the present or the sins of the future, but wholeness reaches back in time to touch and to heal the sins of the past. We are complete in Him.

But, of course, it would be better if we had no need to avail ourselves of this kind of ministry. Prevention is better than cure. And one way to prevent the battering which sexual sin inflicts is to learn to handle the sexual side of a relationship. That is the subject for the next chapter.

9 Touch: A Language to be Learned

'Is there anything wrong with heavy petting?' 'If you can't go all the way before marriage, how far can you go?' 'Is there such a thing as responsible petting?' These questions have been put to us from time to time by couples preparing for marriage.

How would you answer them?

Over the years, Christian leaders have offered their response. Some of these answers have been evasive, some authoritarian, some impractical.

One opinion still being voiced today is the prohibition theory. It may be summed up in two words, 'Don't touch.'

If you follow the advice given by adherents of this teaching, you will not hold hands, embrace or indulge in any form of physical expression of love until you are married. The claim is made that by thus abstaining from touch, a double safe-guard is provided. First, it eliminates the temptation to use touch in order to exploit another's body. Second, it prevents couples placing one foot on a fast-moving escalator, touch, which might hurtle them into behaviour patterns which they would be unable to control. In other words, if you refrain from holding hands and cuddling, your sexual pace will not accelerate to kissing and petting. Self-control will therefore be easier.

In defence of this theory I have to admit that the few couples I have met who based their relationships on it were glad that they had done so. 'I'm so glad we kept our bodies for one another and our marriage.'

But is this the healthiest preparation for marriage? I personally do not believe it is. Is it reasonable to encourage people to demonstrate affection to a cat, a dog, even a pet rabbit, and to refuse that person permission to touch the person they love? This unhealthy view of touch generates anxiety, fear and embarrassment. Too many Christians go into marriage disturbed, even frightened by sex. This results in sexual disharmony. Surely, then, there must be a gentler introduction to sex in marriage, like running in a new car rather than immediately driving it at full throttle.

The prohibitionist theory is frequently counterbalanced by an equally extreme viewpoint. It also may be summarized in two words, 'Do anything.' Any kind of sexual expression is permissible as long as the motive is genuine love. After all, kissing, fondling another's genitals and sexual intercourse are external acts, 'doing what comes naturally.' Why, then, curtail these demonstrations of affection? The outward expressions are not sinful. If couples are not made to feel guilty, all will be well. Remove the guilt and you erase the sin.

I challenge this encouragement to self-indulgent sex. I have already shown in chapter 7 that this kind of thinking is inconsistent with the Bible's teaching on the true meaning of sexual enjoyment. Sex is never just an external act. Basil and Rachel Moss express the real situation with accuracy:

> Any counsellor can testify that sex between human beings, even when intended to be a casual, cheerful gratification of bodily need, or an expression of 'low-level' friendship, very often turns out to be nothing of the kind. Deep disturbances of the human spirit frequently manifest themselves unbidden – passion, adoration, exaltation as well as disgust, hatred, pain and jealousy.[1]

As Christians we shall want neither to trivialize sex, the God-designed love union, nor persons. For love for persons includes respect; it protects their dignity and refuses to besmirch their reputation. The sexual licence which grants Christians the right to exploit another's body in the name of 'love', therefore, must clearly be rejected.

Responsible touch

So is there a middle course? I believe there is. It is the use of responsible touch. Touch is a language which can be learned. It is an adventure into personal awareness, the pathway leading to a deeper understanding of the loved one. It is the wordless language of intimacy.

In this discussion on touch, I am using precise rather than vague language. This lays me open to criticism. Some readers may be offended by my frankness. But others will be helped because they have never heard the issues clearly and openly spelt out before. The wordless language of intimacy is not easily learned in the climate in which we live and using vague or confusing words to describe it would only add to the difficulty. And I believe this language *should* be learned by couples who are growing into love. It should be learned for three reasons. First, because it brings progressive closeness. Just as love draws two people together in emotional, creative and spiritual intimacy, so they should become increasingly comfortable with appropriate physical closeness. Cuddling and kissing should never become a gap-stopper, therefore, a relief from boredom. It will be one of the ways two people say 'I love you'.

Second, touch should be learned because it can be an end in itself. The intention need not be intercourse. Take the welcoming embrace two people enjoy after a day apart, for example. This touch is the language of delight and intimacy. Lust is absent. Is there anything to condemn in this act? Or take the gentle enfolding of two persons listening to music or watching a sunset. The closeness of their bodies reflects the touching of their minds, their spirits, their feelings. Is this wrong?

And, third, the language of touch should be learned because when two people marry they promise to give their bodies to one another for a lifetime of sexual fulfilment. They therefore owe it to one another and the future of their marital relationship to venture into marriage unafraid of touch. But touch is not a language that can be learned overnight, not even on the wedding-night.

But I do not want to suggest that learning the language of touch is without risk. It is as dangerous as lighting a cigarette on a parched prairie in summer. Awakened sexual desire is a hungry flame. It can sweep through the hidden recesses of our being, consuming the whole of us. This greedy flame must be guarded.

There are three guardians capable of controlling sexual desire: the mind, the will and the indwelling Spirit of God. Sexual victories are won first in the mind. It decides, 'I do not want to sin.' The will collaborates, 'I *will* not sin.' The indwelling Spirit of God makes available the resources which the reluctant body then needs to co-operate. So it is possible to learn to touch responsibly. The question is, do you want to learn the art of responsible touch?

If you do want to control the passionate longings which crouch at your door or creep up on you unawares, the subtlety of the temptation needs to be recognized.

Before you consider the art of responsible touch, think about the impact of visual stimuli. They feed the mind. They are more powerful than many of us acknowledge. It matters, therefore, how you dress when you are together. The sight of her boy-friend in very tight jeans might so arouse a girl sexually that she finds it difficult to resist the temptation to fondle his genitals. Men are even more easily aroused by provocative dress: flimsy, see-through blouses, skin-tight tee shirts, low-cut necklines which leave little to the imagination… The resolve to learn the language of touch, therefore, includes the determination to dress sensitively. A person who dresses carefully chooses clothes which are an expression of his/her personality, which are pleasing to his/her partner but which convey the message, 'I am an attractive person' rather than 'I am a sexy person'. It is worth asking one another,

'How do you feel about the way I dress?'

If your partner's clothes make it hard for you to say No, you owe it to your relationship to say so.

Then touch itself is a difficult language to learn, not only for its power to destroy but because it communicates different messages to different people and, worse, different messages to the same person on various occasions. Take fondling a girl's breasts, for example. This might be a man's way of saying, 'I *want* you.' But a man may gently caress his fiancée in this way to communicate, 'I *love* you.' It satisfies his need to explore the body of the loved one and he may have no intention of stimulating her to orgasm. But breasts are erogenous zones on a girl's body. When they are fondled, it sets in motion the process which results in the lubrication of the vagina. This prepares the woman to receive the partner's penis, to enjoy an orgasm. What started as an innocent, loving touch, therefore, could become a hurtful gesture. It is very hard to exercise discipline, to flip the 'off switch' when you have been aroused so deeply.

But this same woman, at a different stage of the menstrual cycle, might enjoy this same gesture and not be so quickly awakened.

Another dimension to consider is that of the maturity of your relationship. The same gesture of love, which may be quite appropriate just before marriage, may be selfish and hurtful at an early stage of friendship or even early in a long engagement. Touch is tricky.

This means that each partner must be willing to interpret his/her responses and to translate them into words. Where necessary, each must be willing to say, 'If you really love me, don't touch me there.' 'If you love me, don't do that.'

This openness in communicating is one of the best preparations for healthy sexual relating in marriage. And before marriage it is a far more reliable deterrent than conscience. Most people can persuade the conscience to allow them to go too far. And alcohol anaesthetizes it. That is why it is so much harder to keep within your boundaries if you have been drinking.

Touch sometimes satisfies our insatiable need to love and be loved. More often, touch unleashes the desire in all its power. We want more. This craving is heightened by curiosity, so couples struggle, not just with sexual hunger, but with the fascination of the presence of the unknown 'which weaves round the sexual act a vast superstructure of phantasy'.[2] It is torment.

When these tantalizing external stimuli coincide with internal fears and bogies, new blockages to wholesome touch are erected.

Take the masochistic streak which characterizes many of us. 'I enjoy touch, so it must be wrong.' And worse, 'I enjoy it so much God couldn't possibly want it this way.'

The God we worship is not a sadist and we should beware of torturing ourselves or condemning ourselves with untruths. The truth is that God is the author of our sexuality. It is therefore good. But, like all good things, sex and touch must be kept in context. Touch is to sexual fusion what learning the Greek alphabet is to writing Greek: the essential preliminary but not the full expression.

To some people, even the alphabet of touch is frightening. Deprived of closeness, denied the warmth of touch in childhood, they fear touch. They run from it.

How do you feel about caresses, tenderness, demonstrating affection with your partner?

Can you give and receive love in this way?

If this is a problem for you, make it a matter for discussion and prayer. Seek help. This is vital, because in the absence of rules prescribed by others, you two must write your own.

Some rules for responsible touch

Before you write your rules there are two things you should do. First, respond to these questions.

In exploring this language of touch, what do we want from each other?

What do I personally hope to receive from you?

What do I hope to give to you?

What will the language of touch add to our relationship?

How could inappropriate touch harm our existing oneness?

Do I touch because I want to convey love or because I am searching for a quick gratification of my sexual needs?

If our relationship came to an end would I look back with shame and embarrassment at what we are now doing?

And would I have hurt you?

Second, weigh carefully the biological factors which might tip the scales, which might persuade you to change the label 'permissible' to 'unwise'.

What does touch do? Touch is to sex what the smell of grilled bacon is to the salivary glands: a powerful stimulant. Holding hands leads quickly to cuddling and kissing. Kissing becomes prolonged kissing. Then the sexual drive gathers force and pushes you into greater intimacies of love-play.

There is nothing wrong with this love-play of itself, but you should recognize that it is the prelude to intercourse. This touch heightens sexual desire. Tactile stimulation of hyper-sensitive areas of the body now produces a very strong reaction. As we have seen, fondling the breasts and kissing the nipples produce a strong reflex contraction of the womb. This prepares the female to receive the penis, to enjoy the crescendo of orgasm. The female body does not easily tolerate an interruption of this exciting adventure into sexual fulfilment.

The male finds it just as hard to stop short of sexual completion. So if touch has caused the normally limp penis to grow, stiffen and become erect, excitement is high. This sexual tension is explosive, almost impossible to control.

If you understand this biological process before you write your rules, love demands that you give the progression of touch careful thought. You must fix firm rules and help one another to keep them. These rules make more sense if you write them before you have started to play the risky game of touch. Back-pedalling is never easy.

Ron and Jill had established their boundaries. They decided that they wanted to reserve intercourse for marriage. That was God's plan. But they faced a four-year engagement and had already indulged in heavy petting, fondling one another's sex organs over and under their clothes. Mutual manual masturbation to orgasm seemed natural and right. But is it?

This common practice whereby each partner stimulates the other to orgasm manually is, to borrow Walker's phrase, a 'mischievous compromise' which may easily produce harmful results.

If you are determined to indulge in this heavy form of petting, which prolongs sexual excitement but separates these physical intimacies from the sexual communion which is their intended goal, you should be aware of the dangers. This practice places healthy sex within marriage in jeopardy for two reasons. After he is married, the man sometimes finds that he suffers from premature ejaculation. The erect penis ejaculates sperm uncontrollably before the penis enters the wife, or immediately on entry. The full pleasure of orgasm is then denied the wife, causing her distress.

Another possible side-effect troubles the husband. It sometimes happens that a woman who has grown accustomed to being aroused in this way prefers manual stimulation to the rhythmical movement of the penis. Normal sex becomes distasteful. But this is upsetting for the husband.

In addition to these long-term hazards, the frustration and nervous tension which many couples experience must be considered. The mind is persuasive. It informs us that the further we go, as long as we do not go 'all the way', the more satisfied we shall be. This is not true. The truth is that sexual stimulation, unrelieved by gratification, causes extreme tension. It causes Walker to conclude: 'the separation of courtship from union and the making of the intimacies that should only act as a prelude an end in themselves cannot be condemned too strongly.'[3]

I shall not easily forget the self-condemnation, shame and embarrassment of couples who have unexpectedly conceived a baby through this kind of body closeness. They had definitely refused to indulge in full intercourse but they had been lying so close that sperm had spilt into the entrance of the vagina. An ovum had been fertilized and conception had taken place. You should be aware that, with this kind of closeness, great care is needed to avoid such an accident. And in those circumstances of heightened arousal you would find it very difficult to be careful.

You should also be aware of the effect of this emotional intertwining of your lives. Just as when two people have intercourse, something irrevocable and deep takes place between them, so this sexual intimacy penetrates the inner self. The dependency and longing for one another increases. It does not make separation easier; in fact it becomes less bearable.

And isn't this a cover-up, a deceit? Can couples who practise this amount of sexual activity really convince themselves or God that they are not sexually one? This kind of heavy petting without intercourse preserves a girl's *technical* virginity, but is it really keeping the rules? If so, whose rules? Certainly not God's. It *may* be keeping to the letter, but certainly not the spirit of God's requirements. It reminds me of the fiction that you can scoot a bicycle along the pavement legally, but you may not sit on the saddle or you'll break the law.

You must decide for yourselves, but if you are seeking my advice, mutual manual masturbation to orgasm lies outside the enclosure, not inside.

How far can you go?

I have attempted in this chapter to make it more possible for you to answer the three questions at the beginning. In my view, there *is* such a thing as responsible petting. It is using touch – embracing, caressing, kissing – in a non-exploitative way to communicate non-verbally, 'I love you.' Wherever that expression of affection exploits your partner's body or your own body, or places your relationship in jeopardy, you are indulging in inappropriate petting. Therefore heavy petting can be wrong. And if you really want my advice about how far you should go in expressing love physically, I would underline five things:

1. Concentrate on the touch which is an end in itself rather than the touch which is the love-play designed to result in sexual intercourse.

2. Avoid provocative states of undress, lying together and over-stimulation of erogenous zones.

3. Learn to defuse the tension by talking to one another about your individual responses to all kinds of sexual stimuli.

4. Avoid being alone together too much and reduce the opportunities for prolonged petting.

5. Beware of allowing physical contact to *replace* other means of communication.

Sexual intimacy is fascinating. Its joys are worth waiting for. Therefore concentrate on sexuality, the differences you bring to your relationship because of the 'otherness' of the male and female. This enriches companionship. Leave the delights of genitality, the fondling of breasts, extreme sexual excitation, until you are married. This gives your mind, your will and the Spirit of God a chance to keep you 'within the boundaries where God's love can reach and bless you' (Jude 21 LB).

I am well aware that this advice is easier to give than to follow. In Galatians 5:13ff. Paul describes how Christians may so live by the Spirit that they have no need to gratify the desires of the flesh. If you are serious about learning this language of touch, read that chapter.

What does it say to you about the problems you face with touch?

How does it make you feel about the discipline you are exercising at the moment?

How do you feel about controlling your sexual desires when with your partner?

Where will you draw the line?

Notes for chapter nine

1. Basil and Rachel Moss, *Humanity and Sexuality* (Church Information Office, 1978), pp.14f.
2. Kenneth Walker, *The Physiology of Sex* (Pelican, 1952), p.93.
3. *The Physiology of Sex*, p.112.

•

10 Planning for Parenthood

'What are your views on contraception? As Christians, should we use it? Are certain methods more acceptable than others?'

These important questions were asked by a young man at one of our week-end conferences for engaged couples. They raise a number of controversial issues which wise couples examine long before their wedding-day.

What are your *views?*
Do they coincide with your partner's?

Should Christians use artificial means of birth control?

Christian opinion is sharply divided on this subject. Some people, notably the Roman Catholic Church, but including a sprinkling of Protestants, refuse to approve the use of any artificial hormonal or chemical form of family planning. Official Catholic policy permits the use of the 'safe period', confining intercourse to the days in a woman's menstrual cycle when she is likely to be least fertile. But a small minority of Protestants block even this concession. As one Christian doctor put it to me recently, 'I believe young couples should just trust the Lord for the size of their family.' He refused to countenance any form of birth control.

Most Christians, however, applaud the use of artificial means of birth control, not for negative reasons, but for positive, healthy ones. This view was well expressed at the Lambeth Conference in 1958:

The Conference believes that the responsibility for deciding upon the number and frequency of children has been laid by God upon the conscience of parents everywhere; that this planning, in such ways as are mutually acceptable to husband and wife in Christian Conscience, is a right and important factor in Christian family life and should be the result of positive choice before God.[1]

The third view arouses widespread appreciation for several reasons, not least because the sole use of the 'safe period' has severe disadvantages. This method of family planning concertinas the joys of sexual intimacy into a very limited space of time (ten to fourteen days each month); a restriction which is to be questioned if we really believe that sexual intercourse is a major means of conveying a special sense of belonging. If it *is* that place where couples feel 'accepted, and accepting, wanted and wanting, desiring and desired'[2], to borrow Jack Dominian's phrase, then why limit this wordless powerful communication to a few days each month?

Enforced abstention is to be regretted for another reason. Sexual pleasure is not only a language used to convey delight and acceptance; its absence frequently becomes a scapegoat for negative feelings: mistrust, bitterness, anger, resentment. When couples are not relating well, their sexual relationship becomes the peg on which they each hang their dirty linen. Prolonged sexual separation can therefore be harmful and disruptive of harmonious marital relating. In my opinion, this abstention is unnecessary.

The Bible appears to support this view. Does not Paul warn Corinthian Christian married people not to defraud one another of their sexual rights? Abstention should take place only if they are both agreed. This should be for a limited period and for the purpose of prayer (1 Cor. 7:5).

It would seem, then, that some sort of birth control is not only legitimate, but necessary. But why insist on the deliberate use of the infertile period to the exclusion of all other artificial means of birth control? The 'safe period' involves a calculated human intervention directed at avoiding conception as much as any other method. So why not allow couples to avail themselves of a choice of contraceptive?

And why shed our human responsibility and shift it on to God's shoulders by insisting that we can trust Him to give us the right number of children. That is rather like walking into the middle of the road in front of oncoming traffic, trusting

God for protection. God delights to protect His children. He also expects adults to behave as adults, to use their common sense and to exercise the freedom of choice with which He invested them. Scientific discoveries have revealed *how* couples may limit and plan the size of their families. Dare we shirk this responsibility in the light of global, familial and personal needs?

And if we recollect the purposes of the sexual act (see chapter 6), several positive considerations push us into selecting a method of family planning which best suits our needs at various phases of marriage. Take the claim that sex is for pleasure, for example. If we believe that intercourse is not simply to create new life, but is also for enjoyment, it follows that we shall abandon ourselves more fully to its delights if we are free from the fear of an unplanned, unwanted pregnancy. Reliable contraception eliminates this dread.

But sexual intimacy has a deeper function than conveying pleasure. It is a wordless language which communicates the depths of love. And more, it is that place where the marital union is deepened. As Richard Jones puts it; 'Sexual intercourse is one of the major means to mediate a dynamic, accepting, passionate sense of oneness.'[3] Couples need to be uncluttered by worry if they are to explore these depths.

Then, of course, there is the awesome experience of conceiving a child, the mystery of pregnancy and child-birth. These events are not interruptions to be endured; they are gifts from God to be enjoyed. But this realization is hard for those who find themselves burdened with an unwanted child or saddled with a string of unplanned pregnancies. The mystery and privilege of co-operating with God in the creation of new life is missed if each unexpected event is accepted with an air of resignation, even fatalism. For this reason, too, the responsible use of contraception is to be recommended. Then something like 90% of intercourse will be for enjoyment and in-depth communication of love. Deliberate attempts to open your marriage to one of God's precious gifts, children, will be comparatively infrequent.

But the Christian believes that all life is a gift from God. Therefore there should always be the willingness to conceive as a result of intercourse. The 'willingness' is not the same as the desire, but it means that Christian couples will rejoice in the 'accidental' conception of a child.

The choice of contraception

Careful thought must be given to the choice of the contraceptive device which you plan to use. The chart accompanying this chapter is a bird's-eye view of the ones most readily available and currently used. More accurate and detailed information is available from the Family Planning Association, or you might refer to Ed & Gaye Wheat's book, *Intended for Pleasure*.[4] There is room here only to discuss the criteria on which to base an intelligent choice

A wise choice will weigh five main factors. First, the *safety* of the method must be examined. Any contraceptive which you plan to use should be harmless for both partners and the unborn offspring. As the chart shows, almost all the recognized methods most frequently used completely fulfil this requirement. Some people dangle a question-mark over the pill. But since this should be taken only on prescription, a good doctor will clarify any doubts you may have about the particular brand he plans to prescribe. He will also reassure you about short-lived side-effects, nausea, depression, headaches, which the pill might trigger off. These symptoms and the allergies which sometimes develop with spermicidal creams should always be referred to a qualified doctor for treatment.

Almost as important as the safety factor is the second consideration: is the method *reliable*? The reason couples use a contraceptive device is to avoid an unwanted pregnancy. You should therefore select a method which is as fool-proof as possible. If it is unreliable, it will not expel the fear of pregnancy and will therefore be counter-productive. Anxiety mars marital sex. It can even produce impotence.

Quite as important as reliability is *acceptability*. By this I mean the aesthetics of the contraceptive method used. Opinions on this vary from couple to couple. Some men refuse to use the sheath, for example, because slipping it over the erect penis interrupts the spontaneity of erotic foreplay

The methods of family planning most frequently used with an assessment of their relative acceptability

Method	For which partner?	Medically safe?	Reliability
The Pill	Wife	Unsuitable for some	The most effective
The cap	Wife	Yes	Highly effective
Intra-uterine device (IUD)	Wife	Yes	Highly effective for most
Condom (sheath)	Husband	Yes	Fairly effective. Best used with cream/foam for safety
Creams Foams Jellies	Wife	• Yes. Some develop allergies	Only fairly reliable. Best used with cap or condom for safety
Sterilization	Husband or Wife	Almost always	Completely, but in most cases irreversible
Coitus Interruptus (Withdrawal)	Both co-operate	Yes	Unreliable
Rhythm (safe period)	Wife	Yes	Only fairly reliable

Acceptability	Availability	Effect
No interruption of spontaneity	Prescription only	Contraception
It must be used with a cream. Some interruption	Fitted by a doctor	Contraception
No interruption of spontaneity	Inserted by a doctor	Is this an abortifacient? Not known
Has to be slipped on an erect penis. Interrupts spontaneity	Chemists or Family Planning doctor	Contraceptive
Must be used immediately before sex relations, often with an applicator	Chemists and Family Planning Centres	Contraceptive
No interruption of spontaneity	Only by surgery	Contraceptive
Results in an incomplete sex act		Contraceptive
No interruption of spontaneity	Temperature charts from Family Planning Centres*	Contraceptive

* The organisation which specializes in Natural Family Planning (*i.e.* Rhythm Method) is The Natural Family Planning Service, 15 Lansdowne Rd. London W11 3AJ.

and spoils it. The sheath also reduces the pleasurable sensations enjoyed as the penis enters the vagina. Other men are quite unperturbed about it and use it regularly. This is why couples must make their own choice. The best contraceptives for most people are those which interfere as little as possible with the spontaneity of the expression of love during foreplay and the resultant orgasmic climax. Therefore most couples prefer methods which can be prepared well beforehand. The intimacies of love-play were not intended to be interrupted or broken off. Fumbling with contraceptives can jar. But, of course, they can be laughed at too.

The choice of method will depend on two further factors. It must be readily *available*. Most contraceptives are. And Christian couples will want to discover the *purpose* of the selected method.

Most contraceptives do what they claim to do: they prevent the union of the sperm cell and the egg cell. This union might create new life: conception. But the claim is made that certain artificial means of birth control are not contraceptives; they are abortifacients. An abortifacient does not prevent this fusion. It allows it to take place, then destroys the new foetus. The effect of the so-called contraceptive is not felt until *after* conception has taken place. This poses a moral problem. If a two-day-old foetus is destroyed, is this the same as abortion?

Which methods are contraceptives and which are abortifacients? Medical opinion is divided. But the only lasting doubt seems to hover over the intra-uterine device (IUD). The way it works is not clearly understood. Is it an abortifacient? Ed Wheat, for one, honestly admits, 'I don't know.'[5]

How do you feel about the use of family planning methods?
Do you need to increase your knowledge of the methods available?
Which do you favour?
What do you think will bring you joy? Which will be most difficult?

Your answer to the last question will not be final at this stage. Couples often prefer one method at the beginning of marriage and then change later. The success of any one method depends as much on individual anatomy and personal temperament as the reliability of the scientific method. For this reason it is sensible to attend a clinic for a medical check-up before your wedding. This has two advantages. You gain easy access to contraceptive advice, and the examining doctor should be able to reassure you if you nurse doubts that normal sexual relations with your partner may not be possible. This early examination may also confirm your ability to have children.

Parenthood
How do you feel about having children?
When would you hope to start a family?
Are you prepared for the sacrifices which parenthood demands?

Parenthood is a privilege. Children are a gift from God (Ps. 127:3–5). They are given on trust. Is there a greater joy in life than to watch the offspring of your love union grow into the knowledge, love and service of their Maker? It is a rewarding experience. Perhaps this was one reason why God commanded the first couple to 'be fruitful and multiply' (Gn. 1:28). God's commands always conceal a blessing, but they make costly demands too. And parenthood is costly.

Motherhood is time-consuming, physically draining and asks for endless self-sacrifice. And fatherhood is just as demanding. Couples who are unprepared to enfold their children in the love which links them should not have children.

Is childlessness, then, a valid alternative? Some Christians feel that the requirement to 'fill the earth' (Gn. 1:28) has been achieved. Surely, then, couples need not have children? Some couples should seriously consider voluntary childlessness where a mental or physical disease might be transmitted to the future generation; this possibility should be prayerfully weighed before God. But the alternative which is not valid is the voluntary childlessness which originates from self-centredness, self-indulgence or sloth. These are not options for Christian couples. If you decide deliberately to deny yourself the rewards which are wrapped in the bundle of babyhood, you need to ask yourselves,

'How will we fulfil the command to be fruitful?'

You might unite in a project designed to extend God's kingdom. True marital love always finds an outlet. The love which refuses to embrace others turns in on itself and stag-

97

nates. But this staleness need not spoil a relationship which God entrusts with the heartache of infertility. This problem is common.

How would you feel if you could not have children?

Infertility is not something to be ashamed of, but the sense of loss and disappointment can be very great. Would you consider adoption? Or would you use imposed childlessness as a prompting from God to undertake ministry which couples with children could not easily cope with? Perhaps you might work in an inner city area, for example. Or offer for the mission field — though, of course, childlessness will not qualify you for missionary work if you are not specifically called by God.

I know all of this is looking way ahead. But there is value in allowing your partner to understand your attitudes, hopes and desires. These views will change with the years. Part of the delight of marriage is watching one another mature and develop. Some of the best mothers I know are those who thought they lacked maternal instinct. They expected to follow a profession. Then God gave them His gift of children, and with the gift came the ability to handle it. But then, isn't that God's way? It is as the Psalmist testifies: 'When we obey him, every path he guides us on is fragrant with his loving-kindness and his truth' (Ps. 25:10 LB).

Notes for chapter ten

1. *The Lambeth Conference, 1958* (SPCK and Seabury Press), p.1.
2. Jack Dominian, *Christian Marriage* (Libra, 1977), p.209.
3. Richard Jones, *How Goes Christian Marriage?* (Epworth Press, 1978), p.88.
4. Ed. and Gaye Wheat, *Intended for Pleasure, Sexual Technique and Sexual Fulfilment in Marriage* (Scripture Union, 1979).
5. See *Intended for Pleasure*, p.154, for a fuller discussion of this dilemma.

11 Growing in Love

How can one justify devoting five chapters of a small book on love to sex? Easily. Even in these 'enlightened' days, Christians are bewildered by the sex bomb. They do not know how to handle it. This widespread ignorance, fear and fascination for sex must be met by firm facts. Christians must receive instructions on how to manage this powerful force so that it does not explode in their faces but rather becomes for them a dynamic force for good. Love is good. But I do not want to give the impression that love is sex. Love and sex intermingle, but they are not the same.

Love in marriage embraces physical attraction, sexual stimulation and emotional satisfaction; and eclipses them. So erotic thrills must blend with the other elements of love. Then, just as clouds shot through with the sun's rays are transformed, love will be adorned. This embellishment of love has a spiritual spin-off. As Paul says in another context, it 'will make the teaching about God our Saviour attractive' (Tit. 2:10).

As Christians, then, we have a double motive for learning to grow in love. This maturity adds depth to our relationships and it brings glory to God.

Are you 'just crazy' about each other, or do you love each other?
What are these 'other elements' of love?

The love of which healthy marriages are made is described in Ephesians 5:21ff.

How do these qualities characterize your relationship now?

The beginning of this genuine love may be detected before marriage. If it is absent during courtship it is unlikely that it will suddenly blossom after the marriage has taken place, though love matures through patient care and attention.

Unconditional love

Christ-like love is unconditional love (Eph. 5:28). Unconditional love is the only love which heals. It is the love for
which you pay no entrance fee. This love is just 'there'. It
declares, 'I am all for you, no matter what you are like at the
moment, no matter what you do.' This is the love Christ
offers to His bride, the church. It is not a blinkered love
which fails to recognize the loved one's blemishes. On the
contrary, unconditional love acknowledges faults, failures
and defects and goes on loving. As someone expressed it to
me recently, 'Rock and Disco music say to a person, "You
are O.K." But God says, "You are *not* O.K., but I love you."'
And unconditional love conveys this same message of acceptance. 'I love you *with* your deficiencies.'

The opposite of unconditional love is deserved love. This
love is not really love at all. It is the reward for good behaviour,
the approval granted only when certain conditions have been
met. This so-called love results in distressed marriages. It
gives rise to doubt; 'this love could evaporate.' It leaves a
bitter taste and gives the impression, 'I am not loved for
myself. I am loved only for what I have to offer.' In the last
analysis, this leaves the partner feeling not so much loved as
used. Do you love your partner, 'warts 'n' all'? Or are you
hoping to change him/her?

Many Christians do go into marriage nursing the secret
ambition to transform their partner's habits, beliefs or life-
style. I remember one bride who paused at the door of the
church immediately after her wedding to whisper to me,
'Let's pray now that he will start coming to church with me.'
In some respects that is an unfair prayer. She married a
non-church-goer. She may long and pray that he will turn to
Christ, but she has no right to demand that he changes his
Sunday time-table just because they are husband and wife.
Unconditional love requires her to accept her husband with
his habitual absence from church. If she cannot accept this,
she should not have married him. Of course, I am not saying
that it is wrong that she should want him to turn to Christ.
But I am saying that if compliance to her every whim becomes
a condition of her love, this is not true love. Neither am I

saying that partners never change. They do. They must. Even God's accepting love requires change in us. But in marriage this change must not be in response to the nagging of the spouse. Rather it must be the inner compulsion of love to love. You change your habits because your love for your partner is greater than your obsession with a particular way of life.

Unconditional love, acceptance without acquiescence, is possible only when love is laced with forgiveness. And forgiveness always finds a niche in Christian love. As Neville Ward puts it, 'Unlimited Forgiveness is what God is.' So if we take divine love for our model, we too must learn to forgive our partner in marriage. This should be neither a duty nor a burden. It should be one of the delights of love. For true love cannot bear emotional separation from the loved one, and forgiving love is love stripped of all pretence.

> Forgiving love is love managing to continue though injured or dismayed or mystified. It continues not by forgetting the injury and dismay or dismissing the mystery to some other world where we shall understand everything but by including it in its appreciation of the one who is loved. This new aspect of him, revealed by what he has done, is understood as part of his reality, indicating perhaps new features of his need, his fear, his mistaken attempt to defend some area of his being from exposure. Where such revelation, though painful, does not produce hostility or even make love more cautious or apprehensive but adds to its depth and equips it for more sympathetic loving – it is forgiveness that is happening here.[1]

This forgiving love keeps short accounts with the loved one. It does not sulk, blame and accuse another. It is not rude and unkind (see 1 Cor. 13:4–7). On the contrary, it suffers for a long time that which it does not like. It thinks the best of the loved one. It 'never fails' (1 Cor. 13:8). But this kind of love is not instinctive for selfish, fallen man. It is an art-form which has to be learned. The only master artist capable of modelling this love is God.

How easily do you forgive each other?

Liberating love

When someone loves you, not for what you are but for who you are; when someone sees the worst about you and yet persists in loving, that person sets you free to become the person God meant you to be. This liberating love is an integral part of Christ's love for His bride, the church (Eph. 5:27). In marriage, this involves drawing out the full potential of the loved one. It includes recognizing the uniqueness of the partner and it necessitates respect. Erich Fromm defines respect in this way:

> Respect means the concern that the other person should grow and unfold as he is. Respect thus implies the absence of exploitation. I want the loved person to grow and unfold for his own sake, and in his own ways, and not for the purpose of serving me.[2]

Ezekiel 16:1–14 provides an illustration of how God, the bridegroom of Israel, loved His bride in this tender, liberating way.

This kind of love elicits a response. It is love in action, love giving. John Newton expressed it well in his hymn:

> Love so amazing, so divine,
> Demands my soul, my life, my all.

To love is to give and to give at cost. True love cares little about receiving; it always rates giving higher than getting. Indeed, not to give would be painful. The model for this kind of sacrificial love is the love Jesus bears for His bride, the church (Eph. 5:26). His love is not so much a feeling as an orientation, a faculty, a series of choices which guarantees the well-being of His bride.

Does this describe the love you have for one another?
What do you need to work at?

Giving love is a caring love. It requires sensitivity, understanding and insight. This intuitive oneness with the loved one not only senses his/her need; it is the propellant thrusting you into the activity which meets that need. To care for someone in this way is costly. And yet, as the Lord demonstrates, sacrificial, caring love is not impoverishment, being cheated of one's rights. It is a sign of inner strength. Erich Fromm puts it well:

> Giving is the highest expression of potency. In the very act of giving, I experience my strength, my wealth, my power. This experience of heightened vitality and potency fills me with joy. I experience myself as overflowing, spending, alive, hence joyous. Giving is more joyous than receiving, not because it is a deprivation, but because in the act of giving lies the expression of my aliveness....Whoever is capable of giving himself is rich.[3]

Sharing love

This giving of oneself to another in love, this sharing, is a vital component of marital love. It, too, receives mention in Ephesians 5:21ff. Just as Jesus literally gave up His life for His bride and died to redeem her, so we must be prepared to lay down our life for the sake of the one we love. In all probability this will not be the sacrifice which leads us to the gallows. Rather, it will be the living sacrifice which lays at the disposal of the other the insights, the sensitivity, the joy, the humour, the understanding, the creativity, the spontaneity and spirituality which are essential parts of one's being. This donating of our whole self to another in unashamed sharing and investment is true love.

This sharing love does not happen overnight. It is a slow, gradual unfolding of oneself in the presence of another. That is why romance should not be rushed. It takes time for this kind of trusting love to take root.

How do you feel about investing the whole of yourself in your partner's welfare?

And does this intimacy want to embrace others? True love is not an exclusive love. From the security of real love a couple reaches out and extends a supporting hand to others. But mere infatuation turns in on itself. It is selfish, miserly and jealous.

How does your love seek to alleviate the aloneness of friends and relatives?

Or is your love turned in on yourselves?

How do you feel about your partner's friends?

That last question is vital for couples who want to grow in love. Some couples cause untold heartache to friends because of their thoughtlessness. Others provide a welcome sanctuary for the lonely single person, as Margaret Evening points out:

> Perhaps those who are married are not always aware how much single people love to relax in the atmosphere of a home and within a family. It is a situation so different from the average bachelor flat or bed-sitter. Perhaps the couple do not always realise just what it is they are sharing with their single friends. For them family life has become commonplace and they have forgotten some of those aspects of emptiness that can be part of singleness.[4]

When we exercise this comprehensive love, we mirror the love Christ and His bride bear for the world. This love is zealous. It pushes the bride of Christ into the entire world for the purpose of drawing others into the arms of divine love.

Unconditional love, forgiving love, liberating love, giving love, sharing love and sexual love. These are some of the ingredients of marital love. In the next two chapters we focus the spotlight on two more: submissive love and flexible love. It leaves couples questioning, 'Who is capable of scaling these heights?' The answer to that is, 'Only God.' The kind of love required in Christian marriage is demanding, almost impossible. Then how does one grow into love?

How does love grow?

This kind of love does not just 'happen', like catching measles. That is a myth of the age in which we live. This love grows slowly, silently, imperceptibly in the same way as the fern uncoils in early summer. But, of course, this unfurling of love requires certain conditions.

It needs persons who have achieved independence. The dependent person does not love in the fullest sense of the word. He/she clings. This clinging vine attachment strangles real love. It also strangulates the partner. As Kahlil Gibran advised, 'Let there be spaces in your togetherness.'[5] These spaces are the breath which is vital to the growth of individuality which in turn strengthens intimacy.

Can you bear to be apart?

Do you need to grow in separateness as well as togetherness?

How will you go about this learning?

Allowing the other 'space' demonstrates a high degree of trust. Without trust, there is no love.

And if your love is to grow, you must each possess the ability to receive love. When you drink in the love which you read in another's eyes for you, it fills you with an intoxicating sense of well-being and worth. It brings security and peace. This openness to relish love is essential. Trust grows, and it brings that deep assurance which every person needs to imbibe, 'I am loved for who I am.' This message rescues persons from becoming a mere statistic on a politician's form or a number occupying a hospital bed. It underlines your value. It is healing.

Can you receive your partner's love? What makes it difficult/easy?

But something more is required. It is not enough to luxuriate in the attention your partner lavishes on you. You must make a response. The mature person savours the delights of love received and takes the next vital step. He/she gives love in return. When you grow in love you cease to view your partner primarily as someone who will satisfy your needs: sexual, recreational, emotional, spiritual. Your partner is not a marital sugar daddy, but someone whose needs can be met by you. And more, if you truly love your partner, his/her needs will be as important to you as your own. For when you grow in love, you are concerned, not so much with seeking your own happiness as promoting the happiness of your partner. To borrow Fromm's phrase, 'love is giving another a zest for life.'

By now it will be obvious that, if love is to grow, the seeds must germinate in the fertile soil of God's love, for only God is capable of loving in this sacrificial way. It is as you each open yourself to the love God pours into your heart for the other that you become capable of this love which is 'other'-orientated rather than self-centred. It is as you as a couple root yourselves in God that you become capable of love in action; the love which by-passes feelings and provides for the needs of the loved one even when feelings are not warm or even particularly loving. God, by producing the fruit of His Spirit in us, equips us to love with the will as well as with the feelings. This promotes the wholeness of the loved one.

This kind of loving is required of every husband and wife whose desire is to mirror the love between Christ and His bride. This love is neither easy to practise nor to understand. As Paul says, it is a mystery (Eph. 5:32). It is incomprehensible. But couples dare not embark on Christian marriage without it.

Is your love a growing love?
Or is it an infatuation which is stagnating?
Do you find it easier to give love or receive it? Why?

Notes for chapter eleven

1. Neville Ward, *Friday Afternoon* (Epworth Press, 1977), p.26.
2. Erich Fromm, *The Art of Loving* (Unwin Books, 1975), p.30.
3. *The Art of Loving*, p.26.
4. Margaret Evening, *Who Walk Alone* (Hodder and Stoughton, 1974), pp.82f.
5 Kahlil Gibran, *The Prophet* (Heinemann, 1926), p.16.

12 Role Responsibility

What are your dreams for your marriage? If you are the woman, do you visualize yourself absorbed in domesticity? Can you see yourself immersed in a routine of cooking, cleaning, mending, ironing, shopping and writing your husband's letters? Do you want to be 'just' a home-maker and the bearer of children? If those questions sound absurd, even repugnant, pause to reflect that they contain a definition of the traditional wifely role. It may not be your idea of womanhood, but it was the style of life expected and accepted by our forbears. Similarly, the husband's role was clearly defined. He was to be the bread-winner, the provider, the protector of his wife and family.

In the past, as we saw in chapter 5, couples adopted these 'spouse roles' without question. A successful marriage depended largely on each partner's ability to fulfil his/her function. Some couples lived together happily; some did not. But intimacy was a bonus, an added extra. Marriage was deemed successful without this perk. Role fulfilment was the make-or-break point of the union.

But today all that has changed. Few couples, if any, marry in order to fulfil a role. On the contrary, couples marry for happiness, for intimacy, for comradeship. Edward Carpenter describes this desire superbly:

That there should exist one other person in the world toward whom all openness of interchange should establish itself, from whom there should be no concealment; whose body should be as dear to one, in every part, as one's own; with whom there should be no sense of Mine or Thine, in property or possession; into whose mind one's thoughts should naturally flow, as it were to know themselves and to receive a new illumination; and between whom and oneself there should be a spontaneous rebound of sympathy in all the joys and sorrows and experiences of life; such is perhaps one of the dearest wishes of the soul.[1]

This desire is the greatest longing of most people who marry today. This yearning seems inconsistent with traditional marriage, and so couples are being encouraged to discard stereotyped marriages like shedding outworn garments. But, as Christians, are we right to strip off our entire heritage? Are there remnants which should and must be salvaged? Is it possible to create a companionship marriage within the well-tried framework of the wife adopting a domestic role while her husband concentrates on providing for the family?

Failure to confront these questions leads to conflict. A misunderstanding of role delineation results, not in the freedom promised by the humanists and feminists, but in bondage. As Christians we shall not want to become enslaved to the world's view. We shall want to adventure forth into marriage with purpose, understanding and flexibility. We must not, therefore, prostitute ourselves to humanist ideology. As God's people, we will start with the Bible's teaching, not man's. We will write our rules in accordance with God's plan, not the world's. What does the Bible teach about fixed roles?

Titus 2:4–5 puts the woman's role in a nutshell: 'Train the younger women to love their husbands and children,...to be busy at home, to be kind, to be subject to their husbands...'. And Ephesians 5:23 crystallizes the husband's God-given role: 'For the husband is the head of the wife as Christ is the head of the church, his body, of which he is the Saviour.'

The next chapter of this book focuses on the question of headship and submission. But what do these other wifely functions entail? And what does this verse imply for husbands who take Christ as their prototype?

The role of the wife (Tit. 2:4–5)

The wife must love her husband. I have already attempted to highlight some aspects of marital love (see chapter 11). This love includes giving another a zest for life. Today, so much emphasis is placed on the urgent need women have to receive education and training to fulfil themselves and find the answer to the 'Who am I?' question, that we are in danger of ignoring man's deepest need. It is the need to feel wanted, approved, applauded by his wife. Irene Claremont de Castillejo puts it well. Young women

> are still buoyed up by the exhilaration of their newly found status. They continue to be wives and mothers, yet are successful in man's world as well. But in so doing they often fail to realize how precarious men feel, and how much the particular man needs his woman to believe in him and to welcome his vision with as much warmth and tenderness as she accepts his child.
>
> He looks to her for recognition of his unique personalness. He does not want to be merely the man about the house, the husband whose duty it is to earn money, and wash up after supper. Perhaps man's need is to be trusted even more than to be understood. He needs to be believed in, and his work, whether she understands it or not, to be given full value.[2]

When a wife fails to believe in her husband, she slowly destroys him and the marriage. I think of one young executive whose self-confidence was eroded by his wife's total disregard for his value and uniqueness. He found himself leading a double existence. 'I am responsible in my branch of the business for the jobs of nearly eighty employees and for the operation of a business turning over a million pounds a year. Do I worry about it? Does decision-making bother me? Do I feel over-burdened or unworthy in that area of my life? No! No way do I feel second to anyone while I am at work. So why do I feel so inadequate as a husband?'

The reason he could not make firm decisions at home was that his wife did not trust him. A lack of trust is also a lack of love.

Are you contemplating marriage? If so,

Wives-to-be, are you prepared to renounce the pursuit of self-actuali-

zation, discovering yourself, striving to keep your career, struggling to centre life on yourself?

Are you prepared to stand by your husband, be loyal to him and support him in his career?

How do you feel about expressing love for him in this way?

Do you believe in him?

And how do you feel about the vocation to motherhood? This is another 'fixed wifely role' which is not only contained in the Bible but which is also a biological fact. The woman conceives babies. This makes inevitable inroads on her career, time, energy, body, hormones and emotions. Are you prepared to accept this role? If not, perhaps you should choose not to marry?

Of course, bringing children into the world demands not just motherhood but parenthood. The need today is for full-time mothers *and* devoted fathers.

How do you feel about devoting your lives to your future offspring?

The husband's role (Eph. 5:21ff.; Ezk. 16)

In the past it was thought that the husband's responsibility stopped at providing for his wife materially. If he contributed an adequate, regular salary and a roof over her head, he had fulfilled his duty. He was a successful husband. This impoverished view of the man's role is unbiblical. As Paul puts it, the husband must love his wife in the same way as Christ loves His bride. This provision is all-inclusive. It is material (Mt. 6:26–32), spiritual (Jn. 3:16), emotional (Ezk. 16:6) and intensely practical (*e.g.* Jn. 13:5). What is this example saying to husbands today?

The discernment of Christ, which recognizes not just the surface needs of His bride but which penetrates into the deep recesses of her psyche to recognize and meet her unspoken needs, must also be imitated by Christian husbands. Just as man has a craving to be trusted, his wife has a yearning to be acknowledged and loved for who she is. She has a need to be set free to become the person God made her to be. This is life; the abundant life Jesus promised. How can a husband draw out his wife's fullest potential?

The secret lies in Ephesians 5:21. This Christ-like headship expresses itself in self-giving. Even the Son of man came, not to be served, but to serve (Mk. 10:45). The pattern for husbands to follow is a superlative standard of self-sacrifice which is unafraid to stoop to do filthy, menial tasks.

Husbands-to-be, are you prepared to assist your partner in the mundane, domestic chores so that she is free to express herself outside the confines of the home?

How do you feel about expressing your love for her in this way?

When a husband recognizes his wife's latent talents and promotes them, he is expressing Christ-like love. When a husband acknowledges the sacrifices his wife makes to create a happy home and makes provision for her to push out the boundaries of her own existence, it is Christ-like love that he is demonstrating. And when a man refuses to leave his wife with heart-wounds that will not stop bleeding, but makes emotional provision for her, he is fulfilling his role as a husband in the fullest sense of that word. Role fulfilment is not task-oriented; it is an attitude.

When both partners allow their attitudes to be transformed by Christ, they stop fighting for rights. Instead, they seek out ways of ensuring that neither abdicates his/her God-given role, that each assists the other in fulfilling this role. Intimacy and comradeship are not excluded. On the contrary, this togetherness is the driving force thrusting the couple into the adventure of marriage, a journey characterized by flexibility in love.

But this attempt to combine warmth, flexibility and God-given roles is a challenge which exasperates many newly-weds.

How do you do it?

One answer is to explore the possibilities of chore creativity. A simple time-and-motion study quickly highlights which domestic tasks need performing daily, weekly, monthly. A flexible couple enjoy deciding who will do which job and when. It can be great fun discovering new ways of coping with chores as thoroughly and speedily as possible. But, of course, this is not just enjoyable, it is also common sense and a wise stewardship of time.

Wise stewardship results in some couples reversing the traditional roles within this basic framework. Take Philip and Mary, for example. Philip makes excellent bread. Mary is astute with figures. While he bakes the weekly batch of bread, she balances the books.

How will your gifts dovetail with each other?

This role flexibility within the framework we have considered nurtures intimacy. It does not destroy it. It is the rigid, inflexible adherence to stereotyped patterns which causes marriages to disintegrate, as Michael and Wendy found.

Wendy was a graduate. After she married Michael she insisted on continuing her professional career. After all, why waste her qualifications? She refused to accept her domestic role. This dismayed her husband, whose expectations of his wife were high. 'My expectations of the way she would care for our possessions, the furniture, carpets, house, didn't materialize. So I used to nag. She wouldn't clean the house. The carpets were filthy. She would never dust the skirting-boards. I even had a tussle to get her to iron my shirts.'

The intransigence of both partners, not lack of role clarification, resulted in back-biting, blaming and the fracture of their union. How could this breakdown have been avoided?

Michael was right to view himself as the provider. The Bible does. He was also right to expect Wendy to care for their home. The Bible does. But nothing was resolved by nagging, blaming and fighting. Rather, love for Wendy would have recognized her need to develop her talents. It would have discovered ways of assisting her so that she could fulfil her domestic role as well as express herself outside the home. But then, Wendy did not help by standing on her rights. 'There is nothing so ruthless as a woman with a cause between her teeth.'[3] And, of course, they could have foreseen some of these problems if they had planned ahead for these early adjustments of marriage.

How do you feel about chore creativity?

How could it work for you?

The biblical norm is that the wife is responsible for the domestic smooth-running of the home; her husband is the provider. Any blurring of these roles should be temporary and mutually acceptable. In the present climate, it is sometimes necessary to reverse these roles, to allow the woman to become the temporary bread-winner if her husband is unemployed or if he is completing his training and she is already qualified. This occasional reversal of normal tasks can be fun, but it can impose a strain on both. And when a wife attempts to hold down a full-time job as well as run a home, she may also become overtired and drained. That is why the current clamour to set women free from domesticity frequently proves to be, not freedom, but slavery to a more tyrannical master. Many young wives collapse physically, mentally and spiritually when this strain is imposed on them.

So wherein lies the source of true marital fulfilment? Zestful, creative, outgoing couples are those who know that the secret of their identity is rooted in God. They know that they were born to accomplish His will for them. Their life seeks to be a living response to the plan He unfolds for them. Two people who unite to encourage one another to achieve this aim do not become colourless people. They become colourful for God; strong, capable, trusted, reliable (see Proverbs 31). They are free.

The world does not recognize this spacious freedom. But as Christians we are often called to run counter to the world's wisdom. We are to become fools for Christ. In this folly of Christ we find ourselves, and we discern that God's purpose is being worked out in our marriage.

No-one forces these roles on you, but they are a part of Christian marriage.

How do you feel about accepting marriage with its role responsibility?
Would you prefer the freedoms of singleness?

Notes for chapter twelve

1. Quoted by David and Vera Mace, *We Can Have Better Marriages If We Really Want Them* (Oliphants, 1975), p.59.
2. Irene Claremont de Castillejo, *Knowing Woman* (Harper Colophon Books, 1973), p.55.
3. *Knowing Woman*, p.56.

13 Love, Honour and *Obey*?

Is it reasonable to expect today's young wife to promise to submit to her husband, even to take a vow of obedience? The world protests against the very idea. It seems deplorable. In recent years the established church has added its assent to this depreciation of the submissive wife, claiming that in the climate in which we live, no woman should be required to make these promises.[1] But are these views right when the Bible so clearly declares, 'wives, submit to your husbands' (Eph. 5:22; Tit. 2:5; 1 Pet. 3:1)?

The submission question is another of those areas where Christians discover that the 'folly' of Christ is their call to freedom. At least, that has been my experience. For years I struggled to break free from the web of requirements I found in the Bible, like a fly trying to escape from a spider. I felt insulted. Ephesians 5:21ff. was a blow to my pride. It seemed preferable therefore to argue the passage away rather than to accept it. Then one day I determined to start with the biblical principle and work from there, instead of reacting defensively and aggressively. Thus I stumbled on the rich mysteries hidden in the submission/headship concept. The headship/submission question is not a coffin bearing away woman's self-esteem and burying a couple's freedom. On the contrary, it is a highway code designed to protect the safety of both partners and to ensure that marriage enjoys a carefree ride.

So what is submission? What are you promising when you take the vow of obedience? Does this elevate the position of the husband? Are you prepared to lay aside preconceived ideas and society's standard as you approach this aspect of Christian marriage?

What is submission?
It is easier to say what submission is not; to dispel the false impressions which have dogged women for centuries. Submission is not the same as servility, subservience or subjection out of terror.

Servility demands a slave-girl wife who is tied to the home as with a ball and chain; whose daily round is arduous, menial, degrading. She is a skivvy. That is not a biblical picture of the submissive wife.

Subservience suggests that one person is number two; that the other takes precedence. This is not the biblical pattern for marriage. The Bible portrays marriage as an egalitarian relationship where husband and wife enjoy a social partnership (Gn. 1:26–28), sexual oneness (2:24), spiritual togetherness (1:26) and a procreative responsibility (1:27). Moreover, Galatians 3:28 makes it clear that in Christian circles there must be no talk of precedence and inferiority. We 'are all one in Christ Jesus'.

Subjection out of fear conjures up the picture of a woman who lives under the thumb of her authoritarian husband. Nothing is further from the Bible's expectation of the marital relationship. Submission does not mean that the wife becomes her husband's doormat. Women who allow themselves to be used, who fail to contribute to the decision-making of the marriage, who think of themselves as inferior to their husbands, have misunderstood what Paul is saying in Ephesians 5.

So what is Paul saying? We need to examine the use of this word submission as it is used in other parts of the Bible if we are to reach an accurate definition of its meaning. The word is used in Ruth 1. Ruth submits to her mother-in-law. 'Where you go I will go, and where you stay I will stay. Your people will be my people and your God my God' (v. 16). Here we catch a glimpse of submission as a positive quality. It is tender and beautiful. It is the deliberate intertwining of your life with another's; love's response to love.

Proverbs 31 highlights another of the positive aspects of submission. This chapter speaks of a wife who was also a powerful woman. This strong woman voluntarily gave her administrative skills, her counselling insights, her quick brain, her practical capabilities first to her husband, then to her children and thirdly to the needy. This is what submission is: a positive yielding of all you have and are to another. Submission, as we see in this chapter, is not playing 'Let's pretend'; let's pretend women are brainless, skill-less, weak. Rather, submission is having the courage to acknowledge one's strengths and to place them first at the feet of one's husband for his welfare, growth and wholeness. Herein lies the crunch, of course. The world persuades us to seek self first. Self-fulfilment, self-indulgence, self-seeking are preferred to sacrifice. But, as Christians, we are called to run counter to this worldly suggestion. And this submission results in the kind of exhilarating, adventurous, successful partnership which the writer of Proverbs implies.

This deliberate self-renunciation is hard. But doesn't love want to make sacrifices? John Powell suggests that it does:

> Love implies that I am ready and willing to forgo my own convenience, to invest my own time, and even risk my own security to promote your satisfaction, security and development.[2]

That is submssion. It is the inward compulsion of love to love.

How do you feel about giving love in this way?

Jesus models this kind of submission with poise and strength. He rejoiced in His unity with the Father. 'I and the Father are one' (Jn. 10:30). This equality did not prevent His ensuring that He lived and worked in complete alignment with His Father's will. In fact, this equality of love ensured that He wanted only what His Father wanted. And this oneness did not blind Him to the paradoxical nature of their relationship. He could declare, with pride, 'My Father is greater than I' (Jn. 14:28). His Father was the head.

Just as Jesus donates all He is and all He has to the Father, so the Christian wife is required to offer her whole self to her husband. For this paradox, equality with headship, extends to marriage. Husband and wife are equals, but the husband is the divinely-appointed chief amongst equals. Is this degrading? Is it demeaning? Is it insulting the wife? Where headship and submission are correctly understood and appropriated, the answer to those questions is an unequivocal 'No'.

Are you prepared to allow your life and talents to intertwine with your partner's?

What are you prepared to sacrifice for your partner's well-being and the success of your relationship?

Whose side are you on? Your own? Or your partner's?

What is headship? (Eph. 5:23)

If this headship were based on power, authoritarianism or dictatorship, then the wife's position in the relationship would be precarious. But Christ-like headship is not power based. On the contrary, its motivation is the self-giving love which costs. The archetype is Christ's headship. 'Husbands, love your wives, just as Christ loved the church and gave himself up for her' (Eph. 5:25).

Thus headship knows nothing of rights to be claimed. It calls forth a superlative standard of self-sacrifice. Headship banishes harshness. Its gentleness draws out the wife's full potential. Headship protects the successful wife and it embraces her when she fails. 'While we were still sinners, Christ died for us' (Rom. 5:8).

Christ's headship over His bride, the church, refuses to dilute the Father's will. Because He is intimately in touch with His Father, because He, Himself, is in submission to God, living a life of unfailing obedience, His instructions for the bride are incisive, accurate, powerful and life-giving. The Christian husband, similarly, is required to listen to God, to exercise his headship by taking the initiative while ensuring that all his plans originate in God. And, of course, the obedience of the wife will never be taken for granted if the husband is, in turn, obeying the Lord Christ; if he is loving his wife as Christ loved the church, forgave her and sacrificed for her.

Headship demands wholesome, healthy, positive, self-effacing love. Submission calls for a high degree of self-sacrifice. Thus mutual giving of oneself to the other is love's strength. It is not weakness. It prompts two vital questions. Not 'What is best for me?', but 'What is best for my partner?' and 'What is best for our marriage?' Two people moving into marriage with this motivation may not succeed all of the time. In partnership with Christ they will succeed most of the time. This mutual self-giving promotes growth. Both partners grow. The relationship grows. This growth is not painless; but then, even growth in nature cannot take place without a struggle. There is inevitable striving and pain involved in growing.

How do you feel about this approach to marriage?
Are you prepared to accept headship?
Which do you feel is the harder role to play?

What makes this partnership so exciting?

A husband and wife who freely donate themselves to one another in this way achieve the intimacy most couples desire when they marry. This closeness is not claustrophobic. David and Vera Mace describe it well:

Marriage...is the intricate and graceful cooperation of two dancers who through long practice have learned to match each other's movements and moods in response to the music of the spheres.[3]

This free-flowing movement between husband and wife is sometimes tender, gentle and gracious; sometimes strong, healthily competitive and co-operative. Neither seeks to usurp Jesus' role in the relationship. They know that He is the Lord of the marriage. Neither over-plays or under-plays his/her own role. They seek a harmony which is life-giving to them, which flows out to others and which brings glory to Christ.

This clarity of purpose and lack of ambiguity add verve to the relationship. Take decision-making, for example. Both contribute their separate insights to the problem in hand. Both submit their wisdom to God's greater wisdom. And in the rare eventuality of a stalemate, the husband has the casting vote. This is not insulting. It is practical common sense that one partner should have the majority vote. The Bible grants this privilege to the husband. Both submit their wisdom to God's. That, of course, is not possible where a Christian partner is married to a non-Christian. It is one of the reasons why you should marry someone who is going the same way with Christ. This avoids the frustration of a lop-sided spiritual relationship.

It frequently happens that a strong, forceful woman marries a shy, retiring man. It seems that she is far more capable of casting the decisive vote than he. Where such wives are prepared to donate their insights and skills to their husbands and their marriages, a beautiful transformation often takes place. Husbands discover *their* full potential. Their ability to lead increases as their wives encourage them to cut their marriage to a biblical pattern. It is one of the rewards of self-giving love.

Are you prepared to donate yourself to your partner and the relation-ship with generosity?

Are you willing for the blurring of the roles which might mean that your partner is praised for something you have planned or done?

Are you prepared to promote male leadership in your home?

In the struggle to do this, what help will you need from your partner?

Compare this warm, secure, creative relationship with the alternative marital patterns being proposed today. Take serial monogamy, for example. Serial monogamy gives a person the right to change marital partners whenever he/she feels the need. Like snakes, it is claimed, we need to change our skins from time to time. But what happens to the emotional and psychological health of one's first partner? Serial monogamy is not freedom. It destroys people.

Or take 'open marriage', the open-ended contract which knows no boundaries to so-called freedom. Couples write and re-write their own contract. Each partner is free to choose the life-style best suited to him/her. This includes sexual licence. This sounds attractive, but where is the security? There is none.

Then there are the pan-scale marriages in which each partner loves only in proportion to the amount of love measured out by the other. But we saw in a previous chapter how debilitating 'deserved love' can be.

These marital styles offer a pseudo-freedom. It masquerades for the real thing, but too often it results in mutual clinging, mutual manipulation and exploitation. The underlying message is that one's partner in marriage exists simply to gratify one's own needs. It is permissible, therefore, to extract from him/her all that meets my need, like a lamb sucking the ewe dry. But these exploitative marriages result in emptiness, not fullness. They create hollow relationships, not nurturing ones. They plunge couples into the abyss of loneliness.

A partnership where Christ-like headship and Christ-like submission are fully operational, on the other hand, brings security, wholeness and warm togetherness. In my view, therefore, it is not unreasonable to expect today's young wife to promise to submit, even to obey. This promise could be her pathway to personal and marital freedom. How are you planning to work at this submission/headship challenge?

Notes for chapter thirteen

1. See *Marriage and the Church's Task* (Church Information Office, 1978).
2. John Powell, *The Secret of Staying in Love* (Argus, 1974), p.44.
3. David and Vera Mace, *We Can Have Better Marriages If We Really Want Them* (Oliphants, 1975), p.5.

14 Ready for Marriage?

Coming together is a start, keeping together is progress, working together is success. If you have worked through to this last chapter of the book, you should have a much clearer idea of whether you two want to marry and when. Even so, the decision to marry is never easy. Ulrich Schaffer explains why:

> I found the decision to marry you
> very difficult;
> I had visions of losing my freedom,
> of being bound
> and not being able to do the things
> I had been doing up to then.
>
> I pictured myself as another nonperson,
> a grey blob in a grey mass,
> just another average guy; /
> I was afraid of not being able to fulfil
>   some of my hidden dreams.
>
> And I was afraid of your expectations,
> your projections and wishes;
> and sometimes I felt that you could only love me
>   because you did not know me yet.
>
> And then I was afraid
> of making the wrong choice,
> because I did not really know what l wanted
> and whom I really wanted –
> And what to hope for in that person:
> I was afraid of the impossibility of backtracking
> the one-way street of marriage.[1]

Understanding the doubts

If you have worked through the questions together, you will have clarified what you want of your partner in marriage and whether it is each other you want. By now the man should be certain. As Paul Tournier puts it: 'When a man tells me he wonders whether he loves his fiancée enough to marry her, I have to tell him that it certainly is not the case. If he loved her with a masculine love, there would be no question in his mind.'[2]

Even so, uncertainties might hover, like the mist which gathers in the valley on a summer's evening. There is a sense in which doubts are to be expected, for important decisions are rarely easy. The responsibility of decision-making often seems formidable and at varying stages of your relationship the doubts will shift from the man to the woman. Walter Trobisch suggests, and I agree with him, that the woman usually 'knows' with a deep, intuitive certainty early on in the relationship that this partner is right for her.[3] Her partner's awareness catches up some time later. But many couples are mystified by the change which happens in the relationship after this initial surge of womanly assurance. Just as the man decides that this relationship is right, that this is the partner he wants to marry, his girl-friend loses this certainty and lacks assurance. She might even decide to call off the friendship, like the girl who came to see me the other day distressed because she had just returned her engagement ring to her fiancé. 'Have I made the right decision or not?'

Does this mean that women are fickle? I don't think so. Paul Tournier puts his finger on the nub of the matter with a fascinating observation:

Nature has willed love to be aggressive in the man and passive in the woman. No one can change that. Love in the man needs to conquer and therefore needs to know what it desires in order to assert itself. On the other hand, romantic literature has abundantly illustrated the paradoxical truth that in the woman's soul there is something that impels her to refuse that which she desires: she says no to the man all the while seeking to be conquered in spite of her refusal.

Normally, her refusal raises the man's desire to conquer...
If... she analyzes herself and wonders if she truly does love him or not, she is asking a man's question, and therefore there can be no answer for her.[4] (My italics.)

It will follow that working through fluctuating doubts requires patience, understanding and a keen sense of humour. But before we move on from the subject of doubt, another observation is worth making. If your uncertainties are accentuated by the climate in which we live; if you fear your ability to create a healthy marriage at a time when marriages all around us are disintegrating, then be encouraged. These fears are to be applauded. They push couples back, not on their own resources but on to God. And couples who co-operate *with* God can create good, wholesome, Christian marriages. I am not saying that God will automatically bathe you in happiness or success. I am saying that hard work on the part of both partners, coupled with the all-sufficient grace of God, turns weakness into strength, even overwhelming success.   •

Do you nurse doubts about your relationship?
What are they?
How do you feel about the observations made so far in this chapter?
Don't ignore them; respond to them.

The hard decision
The presence of uncertainty underlines the precarious nature of relationships. At any time they might terminate. Even though your friendship is serious enough for you to work at the assignments contained in this book, therefore, it is unwise for either of you to form an exclusive friendship with the other. Your other friends and activities are important. They are vital to both of you, whether you stay together or separate. Others need the warmth which you can give them. And, as Christians, no relationship should detract from your prior calling, to seek first the kingdom of God.

Is your relationship in danger of becoming exclusive? How?
Twosomes which leave no room for others rapidly become dead-end friendships. And good, outgoing relationships be-

tween persons of the opposite sex might also lead you into a siding. What then? Supposing you have worked faithfully at the questions I have posed and your doubts about marriage or one another have increased? Or supposing your letters to each other have revealed unmistakable discrepancies? Then you must seek advice from an older Christian whom you respect. It may be that the gulf between you can be bridged; but it is also possible that it will widen. Then you must separate. This farewell will not be easy.

Parting is always painful. C. S. Lewis described it well:

Even if two lovers are mature and experienced people who know that broken hearts heal in the end and can clearly foresee that, if they once steeled themselves to go through the present agony of parting, they would almost certainly be happier ten years hence than marriage is at all likely to make them – even then, they will not part... Even when it becomes clear beyond all evasion that marriage with the Beloved cannot possibly lead to happiness – when it cannot even profess to offer any other life than that of tending an intolerable invalid, of hopeless poverty, of exile, or of disgrace – Eros never hesitates to say, 'Better this than parting. Better to be miserable with her than happy without her. Let our hearts break provided they break together.'5

Feelings may dictate the lie that to allow the loved one to go is folly; but feelings are wrong. The truth is that, despite the pain, the relationship must end.

How do two people cope with the pain of this mini-death? How does one live with the emptiness of aloneness again after the sense of belonging which being loved generates? How do you bind up the bleeding wounds of abandonment? And what treatment is there for the sting of injured pride? Is there a remedy for the scars inflicted by the whiplash of guilt?

There is a hair's-breadth gap between accepting this pain so that you work through it to maturity and wallowing in the mire of self-pity; between resignation and detachment.

You feel empty, lost and alone. Don't deny these feelings. Don't repress them. Acknowledge them. Allow God to move into the hurt and any failure. And just as you entrust Him with your wounds, handle them yourself with gentleness, sensitivity and self-acceptance. This is not a time to blame yourself. It is a time to receive the love of God to yourself. And what does He say in the situation?

He encourages us to be patient in any kind of trouble (Rom. 12:12). His desire is that we open ourselves to His glorious strength at any time when the going is tough (Col. 1:11). Then He demonstrates to us that we *can* keep going, even though our hearts plead that we cannot. Moreover, whenever we have failed, whenever we discover that the seeds of lust, selfishness and lack of self-control reside as much in our lives as in our brother's, He delights to forgive (see Luke 15). This 'bereavement' period, then, is a time for the confession which leads to a glad absorption of the forgiveness of God. Any scars which remain from this severed friendship then become trophies of His grace, not signs of our disgrace.

If you bring God into the sorrow, the tears and the agony, He will teach you a vital lesson of the Christian life – detachment. He will help you to learn, little by little, to unclench your fists from the one who was precious but who was not God's choice for you. I repeat that this will not be easy But with God it is possible to say goodbye. And when you have waved your last farewell, then you must move on to the next thing with Christ. You will embrace the world again.

If that sounds melodramatic, it probably means that you have never suffered the heartache of watching someone you love walk out of your life. It hurts.

The other hard decision

But maybe you have no plans to separate? Maybe you are certain of one another because your feelings whisper the secret that you are meant for one another. Or maybe you believe that God has revealed to you that you are meant for one another. You have no need, therefore, for this book?

Feelings are unreliable and visions 'from God' must always be tested. The revelation might indeed come from Him. But it is all too easy to believe in a so-called divine message if it tells you what you want to hear. If your feelings are right and if this vision is from God, they will be substantiated by the discoveries you make as you prepare for marriage using some of the questions in the preceding chapters.

How do you feel about working at your relationship in this way?

Sometimes when I am walking in Derbyshire I think of couples who stubbornly refuse help with marriage preparation. Towering above the Amber Valley stands a gaunt castle known as Arkwright's Folly. In the early eighteenth century, Thomas Arkwright began to build this edifice for his family. It was never finished, because funds ran out before completion. Now it stands as a monumental mockery. Couples can save themselves the degradation of beginning to construct the edifice of a marriage they cannot complete by preparing wisely.

Are you prepared to work at your relationship, to increase your understanding of one another? How will you go about it?

When Sarah and James spent a week-end working through some of these questions, they seemed radiant. They shared their feelings with me. 'We now feel our certainty is based, not just on fluctuating feelings, but on facts. We understand each other better than before. We therefore rejoice with a deep sense of joy.'

A few weeks later, for they were already engaged, they took their vows. They did not make the wedding promises with cocksureness: 'We know we can do it.' Neither did they accept the vocation to a life of fidelity and love lightly: 'It doesn't matter if we fail.' And there was a complete absence of deceit in their hearts. Neither of them wanted to hoodwink their parents, one another of God. Because their understanding and trust of one another had grown, they stepped across the threshold into marriage knowing that, with God, growing into love was possible. Without Him they would fail. As the Psalmist puts it: 'Unless the Lord builds the house, its builders labour in vain' (Ps. 127:1).

Are you contemplating marriage?

What attitude will you adopt when you take your vows?

Going public

But perhaps you are not yet engaged? If, by now, you know

you want to take the first step of commitment, to become engaged, it is worth considering the timing of this crucial event. Some couples fall in love and want the world to know immediately. They therefore rush into engagement. Is this wise?

There are problems attached to an early engagement. Engagement, like betrothal, is the gateway to marriage. It is the drawbridge which leads to the castle. But it is not the castle itself. Engagement is a commitment with the options open.

Some people question this appraisal. The Bible makes it clear that betrothal spelt commitment, but it did not equal the inevitability of marriage. Thus, when Joseph discovered Mary's pregnancy (Mt. 1:18), he determined to sever their relationship. And Deuteronomy makes it clear that even on his wedding-night, if a man discovered his wife had lost her virginity, he could terminate the marriage contract forthwith.

Similarly, I believe, engagement should be viewed as a serious commitment with a wide-open loophole. Engagement rings are, after all, signs of a loving intention, not handcuffs.

And yet, as soon as a girl wears an engagement ring, parental pressure is exerted. Her mother sets in motion lavish preparations for the great day. Friends bring engagement presents which accelerate the pace. And the personal pressure to fix the date, the church, the reception, speed couples along the road to marriage. Suddenly, a U-turn becomes almost impossible. In my view this is regrettable. Couples miss out on much of the fun of the secrecy of pre-engagement if they go public too soon. They also deny themselves the freedom to work in the way this book encourages if they move into the limelight too early.

On the other hand, Jane and Colin decided to 'go public' earlier rather than later because it was the only way they could convince their parents that this relationship was serious; that they wanted to prepare for marriage, not just enjoy a flirtation.

Which would be better for you – a prolonged pre-engagement with a short official engagement, or a longer official period of engagement?

The other day I stumbled upon an enchanting Chinese

custom which is growing in popularity among Christians in our church who plan to marry. On their engagement day, Chinese Christians attend a church ceremony and move on to this drawbridge of engagement in the company of a few prayerful, supportive friends. This is not a lavish occasion like a wedding. On the contrary, it is a simple acknowledgment that if they are to grow into love, they need God's grace and the fellowship of other Christians. Perhaps that is why Chinese Christians display a banner at their wedding reception. Its symbols contain a message, 'May you enjoy double happiness.' The source of happiness for Christian couples is found within the love of God. A double portion of this joy comes through learning the art of loving each other.

Notes for chapter fourteen

1. Ulrich Schaffer, *A Growing Love* (Lion Publishing, 1977), p.16. Quoted by permission of the author.
2 Paul Tournier, *Escape from Loneliness* (SCM Press, 1962), p.72.
3. Walter Trobisch, *I Married You* (Inter-Varsity Press, 1972), p.8.
4. *Escape from Loneliness*, p.72.
5. C. S. Lewis, *The Four Loves* (Fontana, 1963), pp.98f.